THE SALES CIRCUIT

HOW TO BUILD A LIFECYCLE OF SUCCESS FROM A SINGLE CLICK

DAVID HOLLAND

Cover image by: Yesna99
Book design by: SWATT Books Ltd

Printed in the United Kingdom
First Printing, 2020

ISBN: 978-1-8381902-0-0 (Paperback)
ISBN: 978-1-8381902-1-7 (eBook)

David Holland Publishing
Cheltenham, Gloucestershire
GL51 6PN

CONTENTS

Introduction
Why I wrote this book and how to read it   **7**

01: **Get a quote**
Why a single click ticks two important boxes   **13**

02: **The day it all clicked**
How Janet introduced me to a new world   **21**

03: **Make an offer**
The interface between marketing and sales   **27**

04: **Diving in and branching out**
Tales from Fiji, Hawaii and Grand Cayman   **35**

05: **Sales process**
The critical path that determines everything   **41**

06: **Procter and Gamble**
Persuasive selling and communication skills   **49**

07: **Lead generation**
Irresistible treats for a hungry crowd   **59**

08: **The millennium bug**
How we all bought into a 1000-year fear   **67**

09: **Long term nurture**
Why online relationships lead to sales   **73**

10: **How to Kraft a great message**
Why marketing is a kind of project management   **81**

11: **Client Onboarding**
Create the sale that just keeps on giving   **87**

12: **Counting the cost of winning vs losing**
Why hard-fought victories can end in defeat   **95**

13: **Reviews & testimonials**
Why one third-party word matters more than ten of your own **101**

14: **How I built EXELA**
One small step and one reliable system at a time   **109**

15: **Referrals**
How to triple every sale without even trying   **117**

16: **The final frontier attraction**
How the Star Trek principle can change the world   **125**

17: **Repeat purchasing**
Build an 'existing customers only' community   **133**

18: **108 and counting**
What you do today creates a better tomorrow   **141**

19:   **Build a lead bank**
Back to the top   **147**

20:   **Rinse and repeat**
Shampoo, space and other stories...   **155**

21:   **What about you?**
After all – that is why you are reading this book!   **161**

P.S. Can I help you?   **173**

INTRODUCTION
Why I wrote this book and how to read it

My name is David Holland, and I run a company called EXELA: the leading specialists in using Keap and Infusionsoft to increase sales and save time. This book is about automation: and using it to build an effective sales circuit that will grow your business. But it is also about much more than that – it is about investing in your own life circuit and using your business efforts to create something of genuine value.

The sales circuit

It seems that every single day we hear about 'the journey'. It is everywhere from reality TV and career coaching through to superhero movies and celebrity autobiographies. My problem with the concept of a journey is that it has an ultimate destination – it ends at the end. Don't get me wrong, I am under no illusions that I can live forever (actually I'll live to be 108, and I'll get onto that in chapter eighteen), but I still prefer to view my life as a circuit. The longer I live, and the more I learn about the world, business and success, the stronger my conviction that circuits are the answer. At the very least, circuits are a far more rewarding path to follow than mere A-Z journeys.

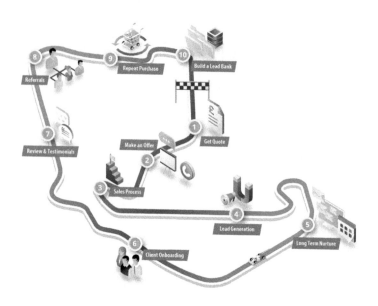

In this book, I set out the structure of a sales circuit and describe how it will build and generate recurring income while also attracting new customers for your business. And we will go on to discover how the automation and processing of the sales circuit will free up your time, mental space and physical energy to pursue your ambitions. We are so fortunate to live in a modern world where technology can reduce the need for manual activity. Yet, so few people have embraced how possible it is to create the life they want to live because of that technology.

So, my ambition for you, while you read this book is two-fold. Firstly, I want to give you insights into the way that automation works, by describing the ten steps of the sales circuit we teach at EXELA. Secondly, I want to show you that it is possible to use the principles behind these steps and the concept of the circuit itself to change your life. This is not a technical textbook, with a list of 'how-to' steps on using Infusionsoft™; so please don't read on thinking that is what you are going to get. It does, however, cover the ten steps, in sequence, and you will learn a little of the process and practicalities along the way. But my real hope is you'll see that investing in sales and life circuitry is worth the effort.

The law of marginal gains was popularised by Dave Brailsford and the record-breaking UK cycling teams of the past decade. It basically states that in any process where one step relates to the next, a tiny percentage change in one step can cause a massive increase to the whole. And in a closed loop circuit, that increase can be both self-perpetuating and substantial. In essence, that is what this book is about.

The life circuit

I have not always been interested in space – in fact, it was quite the opposite. After finishing my academic education and enjoying a fortuitous and adventurous introduction to the business world, I found myself exploring the wonders of the deep. But, as I hit middle age, I started to look up, look out and look beyond what was directly in front of me. Without particularly realising it, I had mastered the art of the sales circuit and how to build a self-sustaining, perpetual, and steadily growing income. My business was flourishing, and I was wondering what next?

As you read this book, and particularly the references to my life experiences, you'll see that I don't like to stick around in one place for too long. And, I suppose that is where my fascination with space was born. It is not that I want to go into space, but more that I believe thinking on its possibilities opens endless opportunities.

So, as you read this book and study the sales circuit that I have learned, borrowed, tweaked and shaped, I want to share with you how it is a metaphor for a successful life. And that the end of that metaphor, like the end of the sales circuit, is the beginning of a chapter where you can think bigger than you ever thought possible.

I know that sounds over-hyped and a little bit fanciful: but you only live once, why not go galactic?

How to read this book

The book has been written across 21 chapters and in sets of two. Each odd-numbered chapter (1, 3, 5, 7, etc.) is about a functional stage in the sales circuit. You should find these chapters educational and practical, and they will be a useful guide to building each of the ten stages of a robust sales circuit for your business. There will also be some tried, tested and proven sales theory contained within these chapters. These are the very ideas and processes that I have learned, used and honed myself over the last thirty-five years.

The even-numbered chapters (2, 4, 6, 8, etc.) will look at how each preceding stage relates to the life circuit. And they will explore the journey from doing a job or running a business to being free to do much more. These chapters will use stories from my own life and truths I've learned from other people's experiences to help demonstrate each point. The final chapter is a little challenge to you to go and do something. If like me, you have read lots of business books, you will know that you often come away feeling inspired but then move quickly on to the next thing.

I hope that this book has a deeper effect on you, and you can see that the things I share here actually work in the real world. And I'd love to hear your stories and ideas about sales, building a better future and reaching for the stars.

Enjoy – David Holland.

CHAPTER 1:

GET A QUOTE

Why a single click ticks two important boxes

When was the last time you purchased anything, anything at all, without having an idea of the price? Maybe, if something was a couple of pounds or less than a fiver, you might just touch your contactless card on the screen without looking. But I'm not convinced of that. I reckon that we all, even if just subconsciously, check the price every time we buy. You see the cost of something is as much about marketing as how much the thing is actually worth.

Even in money-no-object scenarios, or where the price has very little to do with 'why' or what people want to purchase, they will still want to know how much it costs. And any old-school, face-to-face salesperson will tell you that when someone asks you the price of something, they are sending out a major buying signal

Scratch their itch

When a visitor comes to your website to check out what you do or find out if you have the solution to their problem, there is one big question in their mind. How much will this cost?

As you go through this book, you will see that the sales cycle is actually more akin to a customer journey (albeit a repeating one with a beginning but no end). It is all about the customer. To be successful in creating a sales cycle, you need to understand who your customers are, what their needs are, what they want and how to present the solution. And at this stage, when they first arrive at your website – they will want to know how much? Maybe just a rough idea. A ballpark figure. But they want to know.

With that in mind, what is the single best thing you can do for a new customer who has arrived on your website? That's right – give them some form of 'what does it cost' or 'get a quote' button to press.

The other thing that visitors like to do when visiting websites is click on something. So, put a big button 'above the fold' that they can see and click easily. Label the button with words like 'get a quote', 'price calculator', or 'see today's offers here'. This is your first golden opportunity to get a visitor into your marketing funnel – use it.

> **NOTE:** *the expression 'above the fold' simply means being placed in the visitor's eye-line on a website without the need to scroll down. It comes from the days of broadsheet newspapers where the eye-catching headlines needed to be visible on the top half of the page – above the fold.*

You could be reading this now and thinking – what if I have multiple versions of my services, or the price depends on certain factors? I'll come back to that in a moment, but first I want to explore the psychology of the click a little further.

The irresistible click

One of the beauties of the internet is the invention of the click button. A well designed, carefully crafted and skilfully intentioned click button is irresistible to the right visitor. It is like one of those merchandise stands in the supermarket where someone is handing out little squares of chocolate to enjoy or a tiny glass of a new liqueur to savour. People simply love to click. And a clickless website gives off a serious 'do not engage with me – I am not interested in you' message to any visitor.

When I talk to people about a price button, their first objection is often that they need more information before they can respond sufficiently to a client enquiry. I understand that, but the first rule of sales is to give the customer what they want. And in this instance, they have gone to your website to feed their interest in what you do and find out what is costs. So, do that first!

If you are in a business where the price varies according to different needs, you simply need to do what you would in a real-life situation. When a visitor clicks on your price button, you ask them clarification questions to narrow down exactly what they want. Then you could give them the option of going to the relevant page, according to the answers they give. Give them an idea of the costs. Don't be scared to frighten away people who have no intention of buying. Set a reasonable expectation at the beginning of your relationship with the prospect. Make it easy for them to leave their contact details to be emailed the breakdown.

I am under no illusion that you can win business from every single visitor to your site. But I do know that most websites could do a much better job of giving every single visitor the option to 'click here' and start a conversation.

The price motivation

Remember I mentioned earlier how 'asking for the price' is a buying signal? Well, here is the critical thing about getting a click. If you can satisfy a visitor's compulsion to click and offer them the opportunity to give you their contact details, you have landed the perfect storm. You have captured the moment every salesperson wants because they are now ready to start a conversation.

Believe me, when I first got into digital marketing, 20 years ago, this was a much harder step in the cycle. People were nervous about the internet, unsure of what would happen next and very cautious to act. Then there were the golden years where the ping of an email arriving was a delightful sound and building a database of interested contacts was as easy as turning on your computer. As the digital landscape grew crowded and the spammers learned how to weaponise email, it became more difficult again. But today it is easier than you think.

By understanding the motivation of your visitors and responding accordingly, you can significantly increase the number of clicks and contact information captured on any website. You just have to remember they are there because they are interested in how you might be able to help them: but first, they want an idea of the cost.

In a real live sales scenario, if someone asked you the price, what would you do? You would either tell them (if there was a set price) or qualify their request (ask a few questions) if there were other parameters to consider. So, if there is a button on your website that says 'find out the price' wouldn't it make sense to respond to someone clicking it in the same way?

And who, having arrived at a website on purpose because it matched their interest at that given moment, could resist pressing a button that said, 'how much?' or 'best deals' or even just 'prices'?

Now you have their attention

As you will learn throughout this book – finding customers and building a business is done in stages and by creating processes between those stages. This is one of the most important because it is often where a prospect first joins the cycle. It is where you grab their attention – so it matters that you get this bit right.

If a visitor has pressed the price button on your website, they have given you a little bit of their trust, so the next stage is critical. You have to live up to that trust and make sure you deliver an appropriate answer – preferably one that results in them giving you their contact details.

A clicked button is also the opportunity for you to evaluate if the person is right for your business. You do not have to give them an exact price (unless you happen to have a fixed pricing structure), but indicating the ballpark is probably useful. For example, if they have a number like £10 in their head and you are thinking £100, it is probably wasting everyone's time to carry on the conversation. If, however, they are expecting £100 and you are looking at £120, there is room for building confidence and giving the interested party more reasons to engage with you.

As we leave this first chapter, I want you to remember one crucial thing, and bear it in mind throughout the rest of the book. If a prospect has expressed an interest in what you do, you owe it to them to try and satisfy that interest. And, if you do it the right way, you can start a fully automated, genuine and mutually beneficial conversation that could lead to a lifelong business relationship.

In the next chapter, I will share a little more about my story and how my relationship with sales automation cycles started with a single click. I hope that you will glean some valuable insights and lessons from my early experiences and introduction to business life.

CHAPTER 2:

THE DAY IT ALL CLICKED

How Janet introduced me to a new world

Having finished school with several O-levels (GCSE equivalent for younger readers), the subject that attracted my interest the most was biology. I found things like the Krebs cycle and oxidative phosphorylation fascinating, and this topic was perhaps one of my earliest introductions to the idea of cyclical events. In straightforward terms, it describes the way that citric acids play a part in the respiratory system of all breathing organisms. But the relevance to this book is that it wasn't a simple A to B journey. It is a pre-set and perpetual cycle that just keeps on going as long as the organism is alive – just like a strong automated sales and marketing circuit.

I'm not sure I ever had any ambition to become a biochemist. I was, I suppose like many kids straight out of school, still working out who I was as much as knowing what I wanted to do with my life. But biochemistry did interest me enough that it became the degree I chose to study. That decision took me to Dundee University in the summer of 1982 (I say summer, but for those of you who don't know – Dundee is in Scotland where that season can be elusive!)

While I was there, I investigated a few other activities on the campus and tried out several sports clubs and events. I suppose you could say I was visiting sites to see if any of them would feed my interests. Again, like with the biochemistry course, I chose the thing that I found the most engaging and joined the karate club. In fact, being a bit of a compulsive organiser, I eventually took over the running of the club. News of my endeavours soon reached the ears of a guy called Brian Drome who asked me if I would like to take over from him as the President of the Sports Union in my penultimate year. I suppose I had sort of fallen into these various positions, places and roles purely by following and responding to my own interests.

What interests you?

Before going on with the story of how I met Janet, the person who launched me on the trajectory that I find myself on today, I want you to ask yourself a question. I assume, if you are reading this book, that you are either a small business owner, a marketing manager or someone whose role includes trying to generate new business for your company. If my assumption is correct, one of the most essential skills you could invest in developing is how to identify people's interest and motivations. And a great way to do that is to start with yourself.

Ask yourself how you got to be where you are today? And I mean quite literally sitting where you are, travelling towards whatever destination is in front of you. My guess is that you are either there because you have followed things that interest you or you have been driven by necessity. And if it is the latter, and you don't really want to be doing what you are doing right now, it is simply because that interest has not developed yet or it is not strong enough to drive you. People are creatures of habit and will take the route of least resistance or follow their dreams.

And the lives of the thousands of high-flying executives, industry experts and brilliant entrepreneurs who I have had the honour to meet over the decades tell me one thing. If you let the things that interest you drive your life – you will go far. That, in essence, is why I believe you owe it to people whose interest has led them to your website, to allow them to click something and learn more.

Back to Janet and the turning point

So, there I was at university, studying for a degree in a subject that I found interesting but had no desire to pursue for life, and thoroughly enjoying organising the Sports Union. One day, I got invited to see Janet, the university's Careers Officer. I explained to her what I was thinking and that I didn't really know where to go from there. Little did I know, at the time, that she was also a spotter for Procter and Gamble and tasked with finding talent for various roles within its global consumer goods empire. To be honest, I hadn't even heard of Procter and Gamble at the time, but I clicked the metaphorical button that was offered to me and went for the first interview.

A guy called Mike Ashton came up to the university and interviewed me for an hour or more. He then invited me to go to Glasgow a week or so later for a second interview that lasted six hours (yes – six). Then they asked me to travel down to Newcastle to spend a morning with an Area Sales Manager, before being passed into the hands of Keith Dickens, the Divisional Manager for the rest of the afternoon.

By the end of the afternoon, Keith offered me a job. What impressed me the most about the whole process, and the reason that I am sharing the story here is that at every stage of that process, the person responsible had the authority to tick the box. Janet knew precisely the type of person they were looking for. Mike was qualifying her recommendation in the first meeting and clarifying other criteria in the second. The Area Sales Manager had his list of benchmarks and measures, and Keith had the ultimate responsibility of signing off the deal. Something to consider is that Janet was clearly the junior decision-maker here, but without her, none of the other stages would have happened, and I might be in a very different place today. Thank you, Janet.

When you come to design your sales and marketing circuit, I would encourage you to bring this little story to mind. Better still, think back to the last time you made a significant buying decision like buying a car, moving house or taking on a new employee. What were the checkpoint verifications and clicks (or 'yes' buttons) that needed to be ticked along the way? It is exactly the same for your sales circuit, and deep thought about the process will pay for itself many times over I promise. And don't forget that it often all starts with a Janet button saying 'click here'.

Imagine what would have happened if I had told Janet I was dead set on becoming a biochemist, and she had still put me forward for the role. Do you think Mike would have appreciated driving all the way up to Dundee to interview a dud? And what if the next person she contacted him about was equally unsuitable? Do you think they'd have given her many more chances to get it right? As far as I can tell, Janet offered the click button to people who were ready to click. So, make sure your click button is telling the right story.

CHAPTER 3:

MAKE AN OFFER

The interface between marketing and sales

Broadly speaking, sales and marketing are part of the same sales circuit, and the overlap is inseparable. The gap is even tighter in an online, automated sales process than when selling in person. For argument's sake, however, here is a brief definition of the two:

> *The role of marketing is to identify and collect leads by sharing information and creating an interest in the products and services that a company has to sell. The sales part of the process attempts to convert those interested leads into paying customers. In straightforward terms, you do that by making them an offer – because if you don't offer them anything, they are never going to buy it.*

What is the motivation?

Let's imagine that you have earned a click. It might be the price button that I mentioned in the first chapter or a request for more information about a particular subject or product on your website. But there you are with an email address of someone who has shown a genuine interest in what you do. That is valuable, and you do not want to mess up this opportunity. So what can you offer them next?

It may be that you have products to sell and your sales process is as straightforward as that. All you really want is for them to indicate how many they want and go to the checkout. If that is the case, there is still a lot more you can learn from this book; about attracting prospects, turning first-time buyers into lifetime customers, generating referrals and building a lead bank. But for now, let's assume that this click is the first stage in a selling circuit: and the next stage is to see if they will take or make a phone call.

So, what would be the thing that makes them want to take that action? What is their motivation for being there? And how are you going to capture this opportunity? You might only get one chance at this point in the cycle: and in many ways, this is one of those make-or-break areas. At most other points in the sales circuit, you have a second chance if you get it wrong, or you have a bit more time to guide them to the next stage – but this is a crucial step.

So you'd better make sure that your offer is good one. And a major aspect of achieving that is to make it extremely easy to execute.

Action or Reaction?
Which is easier?

So, let's look at lead magnets: what they are and how to use them. In simple terms, they are various forms of valuable information that a visitor to your website can download in exchange for their contact details. The key to creating a good lead magnet is to make it both desirable and valuable in a visitor's eyes. In short, you have to make them want it enough that they will allow you to add them to your list.

Ask yourself: which would be the easiest objective to achieve? Getting a visitor to your website (one who you have never met or spoken to before) to pick up the phone and call you? Or talking to them at an event? Yes, I agree;

the first action is going to be more challenging than the second. So, don't do what most people do and simply give them that option. Create multiple opportunities for you to get into a conversation with your prospects or to move them along the sales pipeline towards a close. Reactions are easier to create than proactive actions.

Your offers should range from calling you to discuss their needs or booking a slot in your diary; through to joining your live webinar or meeting you at a trade show.

Landing leads in your pipeline

The two primary components of the pre-sales process (lead generation) are creating lead magnets and choosing a (or a variety of) lead capture mechanism(s).

Lead magnets are content or assets, usually given away for free in exchange for data that will allow you to contact the person again. The purpose is to create something that your ideal market (avatar) will see as valuable or useful and feel compelled to accept the offer. They will be fully aware that in making the exchange they are inviting you to market to them: so, the value you give them must be all that it claims to be.

It will need to speak to a pain they are experiencing, answer a question that you know they will ask, offer to make their life easier, or a future purchase more advantageous. Think carefully about the sort of thing you can put together and how you can create as much real and perceived value as possible in your offer.

In chapter seven, we will dig a little deeper into lead generation, and how to attract multiple streams of new prospects into your pipeline. Perhaps when you get there, you might want to come back to the following list. I think you'll then realise just how powerful having first identified your market is in the whole process.

Here are some ideas for effective lead magnets that you could create:

- Reports: business-critical information about the sector; or you could make this report specific to the individual after asking them a few clarification questions

- Free consultations: you are the expert and, hopefully, the content on your website has persuaded your visitor of that fact; so offering them a free 1-2-1 consultation with you may be very attractive for some

- Checklists: if you understand how to do something that your prospects would like to learn, there are few things more compelling than simple step-by-step instructions and a checklist to make sure all the bases are covered

- Free samples: sending free samples, or a try-before-you-buy offer, is a great way to let your prospects test out your products – it also demonstrates that you have confidence in what you have to offer

- Books and eBooks: publications of any sort tell prospects that you are an expert and build your credibility with that person – also, they get to read up on your story and expertise while appreciating your free gift

- Vouchers: taking the sting out of a first purchase by offering generous discounts or coupons is a powerful tonic

- Email series: sending a series of weekly or even daily emails with a step-by-step guide or drip-feeding valuable information is a useful way to generate a string of engagement – done well, and to the right people, this can create genuine anticipation among people who will look forward to seeing what they will receive next

- Video series: this creates a similar reaction as an email sequence, but often gets a higher response rate and is more engaging for most readers

- Seminars and online training: as mentioned in chapter four, these are often the best type of lead magnet because they create an environment where you can engage with your prospects directly and in person

Another point to remember with lead magnets is that you do not need to be limited to just one format. You can try various methods and see which works best, or you may discover that a two or three-pronged approach is the best option.

There are various **lead capture mechanisms** you can employ to make your lead magnets available to your leads. This is the actual system that will both deliver your lead magnet and capture the lead's information. Without this, you cannot build that all-important lead bank that you need to start feeding leads into your pipeline.

Here are some typical lead mechanisms that you could use:

- Landing pages: a single webpage/domain explicitly designed to capture a prospect's data

- Webform: a page on a website where an interested party can input their data

- Inbound email: where the lead responds to an email with their contacts information

- Inbound SMS: like the email response but through an SMS or text message

- Messenger(s): inputting a lead's contact data through a social media service such as Facebook Messenger

- Business reply: an old-school postal 'by return' system of collecting a prospect's contact data

- Freephone numbers: using telephone numbers to track and capture callers' details

As with the magnets themselves, you are not limited to one of these systems. In fact, I would encourage you to experiment with as many as you can and employ multiple methodologies to bring in as many leads as your sales process can handle.

CHAPTER 4:

DIVING IN AND BRANCHING OUT

Tales from Fiji, Hawaii and Grand Cayman

I was at Proctor and Gamble for about three years and left a completely different person to the commercially naive graduate who had found himself placed there. I will always be grateful for what they taught me and will share a little more information about their sales philosophy in chapter six.

But, in November 1989, I decided to take a year out to go travelling. My plan, if you could call it that, was to head towards Australia; but I hadn't really worked out why I wanted to go there, or even how. I bought a ticket to Istanbul and Delhi, just because they were places that I had always fancied visiting. Turkey met my expectations and was as magical and exciting as I'd ever envisaged it would be. I didn't particularly enjoy India, although I'm not sure I could tell you why, and maybe if I went there again, I'd feel differently. Next, I whizzed through Thailand, Singapore and Papua New Guinea; then stopped off in Hong Kong before eventually landing in Brisbane.

I hear so many stories of other young travellers who set out to reach a specific place and never arrived having found a more exciting and fulfilling destination along the way. I suppose, as we've just covered in the last chapter, the marketing of all those countries I sailed through, sometimes no more than a week at a time, didn't appeal to me – so I never committed to buying into their offer. Or maybe it was just that I had my heart set on Australia, and that was where I wanted to go.

As I mentioned earlier, I believe that if I were to follow the same path today, there would be dozens of things that might catch my eye, steal my attention and maybe even turn my heart. But back then it all pretty much passed me by. That, in essence, is why the sales automation circuit I'm teaching you in this book is a cycle and not a journey. The more times you reach the same people, the better the chance that you'll catch them at the time when they are ready to buy.

Australia and why it didn't work for me either

So, I found myself in Brisbane, early in 1990, and from there I travelled down to Sydney, although that too was more a choice of going North or South than particularly knowing where or why I was going.

In Sydney, I settled down a little and got a job in the Hofbräuhaus House under the iconic Sydney Harbour Bridge. I 'almost' fell in love with the New South Wales and German beer vibe, but the call to explore still beckoned. After three months, by far the most prolonged stay of my trip to date, I loaded up the Ford Econovan camper van I had bought and headed westward. Norman and I (that was the name I gave the van), took our time and enjoyed the stunning Australian countryside and seascapes as we journeyed via Melbourne, along the Great Ocean Road and arrived in Adelaide. From there we travelled north along the Stuart Highway through Coober Pedy and Alice Springs, and then on up to Darwin.

I worked in Darwin for a while, more to build up funds than because it was any better than the other places I had visited. From there, Norman took me west and south again to the beautiful city of Perth. While its attractions; the Swan River, King's Park and Rottnest Island; were many, I still hadn't seen enough to tie me down. But I did take a PADI open water scuba diving course while I was there – and that, perhaps, was my first bite at responding to a call.

The open road beckoned again, and there can't be too many roads on earth more open that the Eyre Highway across the Nullarbor Plain. At 1660km long, including the longest stretch of straight road in the world, this journey is one I would sooner forget. Norman too would never be the same again and thirsted for as much oil as he did petrol in the days it took us to get to back to Adelaide. Poor Norman.

After enjoying the thrills and spills of the Australian Grand Prix in Adelaide, I headed off to Queensland again and ended up in Townsville (a long way north of Brisbane).

There I took my newfound diving passion to another level – qualifying as a rescue diver. And that was the end of my Australian adventure.

But I was certainly getting deeper into the diving vibe.

Waikiki beach and falling in love – twice!

Having read the last few quick-fire paragraphs, you'd be forgiven for thinking that I simply didn't have it in me to settle down or that I was easily distracted. The fact is that I didn't know what I was looking for, but I knew I hadn't found it. I had, however, discovered a love of diving, and at every opportunity, I was determined to learn more.

After Townsville, I travelled to Fiji where I passed my divemasters qualification; and then I jumped on a plane to Hawaii and became a fully-fledged dive instructor. It was here that my passion for diving quenched my thirst for travel. From testing the water in whatever location I found myself in, I decided to settle and start lapping up the life and the opportunity. And I also reconnected with the entrepreneur that Proctor and Gamble had uncovered and started to make serious money once more.

I got a job in a hostel called Hawaiian Backpackers and, along with a few of the other guys, we were effectively running the place. I also worked for a guy named Bruce Basser, who ran Beachdivers Hawaii, taking tourists out on his luxury six-person dive boat. At the time I started working for him, the business was only just getting by, so I started selling dive experiences to the backpackers passing through the hostel. Pretty much every day for the first three months I was there, I would bring Bruce two, three or sometimes four punters to fill his boat. I would then run the diving trips for him and effectively kept his business afloat.

From there, I teamed up with Karim, a guy I'd met during my instructor course. Karim was an acupuncturist and ran a business taking people sailing in his catamaran, from Waikiki Beach. He also had some rental dive gear, so I would pay him a small leasing fee to take out groups each day on his boat. Cutting out the middleman, I suddenly found my sales efforts were putting a relative fortune in my pocket – plus I was getting to dive in Hawaii every day – for a living. I had found my element.

Then one day, while taking a bit of time out on Waikiki beach, I met my future wife. Jacqueline and I hit it off straight away, and the meeting had an air of destiny about it, but she soon left for China and (we kept in touch, but) the next time I saw her was back in the UK.

Settling down and buying back into life

Early in 1992, I went back to the UK for a friend's wedding and, knowing Jacqueline was also home; I invited her to be my plus one. She had landed a marketing job at The London Rubber Company, so she committed herself to her new role there, and I flew out to the Grand Caymans for another nine months as a scuba instructor.

By 1993 I'd got the travel bug out of my system and decided to come home, staying with a mate in Sandbach in Cheshire. Jacqueline moved across and started looking for a teaching role (marketing, it turned out, wasn't her thing), and eventually she got on a teacher training course at Gloucestershire University, in Cheltenham.

Meanwhile, my first venture into getting a proper job took me to Kraft Foods, also in Cheltenham in a sales role. It seemed fate had brought us together and we were married in August 1993.

CHAPTER 5:

SALES PROCESS

The critical path that determines everything

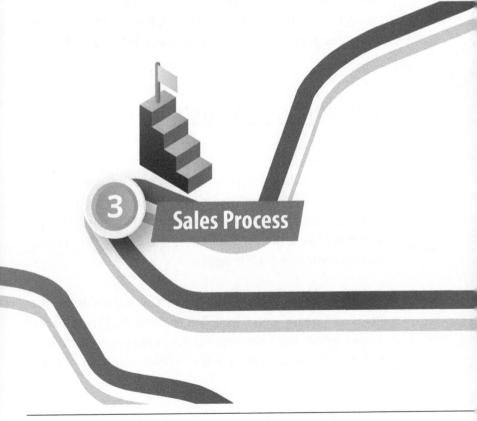

3 Sales Process

In sales, we use the leaky bucket analogy in two ways. Firstly, there is the example of existing customers leaving a business and going elsewhere because the company has taken them for granted by not paying them any attention or giving value. In this version the bucket represents your revenue: but, while you work hard to keep it topped up, just as much is escaping through the holes. It is not a pretty picture and is a totally avoidable and unnecessary scenario.

I will cover how to fix this first type of leaky bucket in the chapters on 'long term nurture' and 'repeat purchase'.

Here, I want to examine the other type of leaky bucket – although it is better described as a leaky funnel. This version addresses the leads fed into your sales pipeline but which slip through the gaps, seep out the edges or pour through the holes as rapidly as they came in. This too is an ugly picture, but the good news is that it is just as solvable.

A leaky bucket costs you money

It simply doesn't make any sense to spend money generating leads without being sure your sales process consistently converts opportunities into deals. If your process is not working efficiently, it would be wiser just to turn off the tap and start fixing the problems. It is the proverbial pouring money down the drain in action.

The important thing is to identify where in the process the leads are being lost. There are various stages and sub-stages within any sales process, from the point that a lead enters your sales pipeline to the decision to buy or not. But it only takes one gap to create a potentially expensive hole. These gaps can only be plugged when you fully understand your process – from start to finish.

In the last twenty years, I have studied dozens of methodologies, from sales gurus to psychologists, and each one has a slightly different perspective on the same subject. They all describe variations of the elemental step-by-step journey that a salesperson (or automated system) must walk their prospect through before they become a customer. You could stop reading this book now and spend the next twenty years doing similar research to me – but I promise you that you'd summarise your efforts in a similarly simple way as I am about to describe.

The simple four-step sales process

The key principle that underlines the steps that follow is that a good salesperson (or your automated sales system) must continually control the conversation while responding to the needs of the prospect at every stage.

Stage one: Qualification

You need to devise a way of qualifying each lead that enters your sales pipeline. If you are going to invest time and money in trying to convert a lead into a customer, you will maximise your return by concentrating on the ones that are more likely to convert quickly. For example, if you are trying to sell scuba-diving gear and your lead base is everyone on the beach, you might start by asking people if they have dived before. This qualifying question would give you an indication of each individual's likely need or desire for your products.

Of course, you could try and sell to everyone in the hope that you might capture the attention of some first-timers. But your percentage hit rate would be lower, and even those that were keen would be more likely to hire than to buy for their first lesson. Selling to everyone will cost more in time, money and effort than selling to the qualified group of people who are more likely to have a need.

Average salespeople with a well-qualified lead base will outperform the best salespeople with a random one every single time.

Stage two: Discovery

Time now needs to be spent with each qualified lead to discover their specific needs and requirements. Think of this as a deeper stage of qualification and understanding. During this stage, the salesperson will be looking to establish who makes the buying decision, their current situation, if there are any other issues to cover, whether the need is immediate or for the future, and what the prospect's ideal outcome looks like.

Following through on the scuba-diving example; you will identify any prospects who have attained a level of certification and decided they want to go diving again. Diving is all about the experience and what you see underwater. Merely asking the prospect what they hope to get out of a dive with tell you if your dive adventure is right for them. Of course, you could discover that the prospect is looking for something different and has no interest in your products. Letting them out of the funnel at this point is not seen as a leak, but rather an opportunity to invite them back in the future when the time is right for them.

Stage three: Bidding

In chapter seven, covering 'lead generation', I will make the point that 'selling is easy' if you have executed all of your preparation work well. That is relevant here too because if you have qualified your leads, dug further into their needs; and identified specific areas in which you can help them, it all comes down to delivery and cost.

So, stage three is about submitting the quote or bidding for the work. Most people get this stage confused with only providing a cost for the job, and that is why a lot of opportunities find their way to a hole in the funnel at this point. The expression 'always be selling' is important here, and you must take the opportunity to reinforce the buyer's decision.

If you have been thorough in stages one and two, you have every right to approach this stage with the assumption that your prospect wants what you have got. So, while informing them of the price of doing business with you, remind them of what you are going to deliver. Your quote should include details of what they are getting, how it will be delivered, when it will arrive, and who will be responsible for making it happen.

Stage four: Closing

If we break these stages into percentages of influence, this one represents just 10% of the action, but 90% of the importance. If you have qualified a lead, identified that prospect's requirements, and pitched an ideal solution at the right price, closing the deal should be little more than a formality. And yet, it is where most sales fall through.

Whether it is asking for the business, getting a signature or agreeing on the start date and taking the first payment, salespeople are notoriously bad at closing. The great thing about automation is that the critical final push is simply part of the process and doesn't require an uncomfortable pause or battle of wits.

The good the bad and the ugly of sales scripts

For each stage of the process, a salesperson needs a script or plan. For some people, or in some scenarios, this might take the form of a word-for-word monologue. For others, it will be a loose framework that needs to be followed or adapted to a personal style. But even for the most skilful, fluent and experienced salespeople, a general roadmap of the points that need to be covered is essential in keeping the sale on track.

In an automated sales process, each stage will be carefully crafted, tested and tweaked to discover the most effective method for walking a lead from one end of the funnel and into the customer pool. This will probably start with some sort of PPC (pay per click) advert: then lead them through a sequence of small steps of engagement (emails, messages, post, gifts, information and other valuable communications) until they are ready to buy.

Generally speaking, the bigger the purchase, the more complex and greater level of thought that needs to go into the sales process. But every sale will follow a similar path to the four steps described in this chapter.

Carefully crafted, premeditated scripts are critical because they control the path and ensure that important points along the way do not get overlooked. For example, if you move into the qualification stage without having first established that your lead is even in the market for your products, you are wasting everyone's time. And, if you have not built up enough rapport and trust with your prospect before pitching a price to them, your risk of losing the sale increases significantly, even if you have the best possible product at the lowest cost.

In chapter 10, 'How to Kraft a great message', I will share some of my views on storytelling for business and the secret to using it as an effective sales and communication tool.

CHAPTER 6:

PROCTER AND GAMBLE

Persuasive selling and communication skills

In chapter two, I told the story of Janet starting a sequence that led to my career with Procter and Gamble. Early on in my time there, in 1986, I was taught two fundamental skills that have served me well in life and in business ever since. While they are not specifically about online sales generation or building a technology-driven based communication cycle, they are the most powerful sales and communication techniques I have ever learned. I hope you will take even a small bit of wisdom from this chapter, to help you in face-to-face selling and communication scenarios, but I will also reference why these skills are relevant to automation at the end.

As I said, I learned these skills 35 years ago, and have been practising and perfecting them ever since. I went on to work for several other global corporates and benefited from their training, culture, processes and methodologies. But I have never found anything to be stronger or more effective than the communication skills that Procter and Gamble taught me.

What I learned from P&G

During my first week with Procter and Gamble, I was packed off to a hotel for three days with other new starters from that year's graduate intake. Firstly, we were taught the fundamentals of **effective communication**: covering both listening and speaking (in that order). Then, after we had gone through all the basics in a classroom situation, we spent a whole day practising, critiquing and fine-tuning what we'd learned in roleplay scenarios.

On the third day, after becoming familiar with communicating effectively, we moved our focus to the other skill that has stood me in good stead ever since: the art of **persuasive communication**, which is also known as selling. This was an absolute revelation to me back then and, 35 years later, I still marvel at the sure and certain infallibility of the results.

In this chapter, I am going to share an outline of what I learned from Procter and Gamble.

Open the blinds and let the communication begin

As we go through this information, I am going to describe it in reference to a window with a blind (the pull-down type that blocks out the sun). We called it the Johara Window, after the two psychologists, Joseph Luft and Harrington Ingham, whose work on relationships between people inspired it in 1955.

In simple terms, the idea is that you are consciously and deliberately trying to open the blind (in effect the communication channel) to the person or people you are speaking with. Some actions, or verbal statements, will tend to close listeners' blinds, while others are more effective at opening them.

You open the blinds in stages by being friendly and open.

- **General statements:** These should be designed to set the scene and make it clear why you are there, and the reason that the conversation is taking place. They should always be positive, or neutral statements and are based on relevance to the occasion; rather than simply asking about the weather or their weekend.

  "Let's begin by getting a better understanding of your current situation" or *"Our role, moving forward, will be to help you identify and achieve the things that are most important to you."*

- **General leads:** Whereas you start the communication by making statements about the purpose of the conversation, you then need to start leading the other party into stating what is important to them. Think of these as open questions – you are, after all, encouraging them to open their blind.

"Tell me more about that?" "What are you looking for from this?" or "How can I help you with that?"

- **Pause for more:** I implore you to try this the next time you are talking to someone – just to see how powerful it can be. It is almost like a magic trick if you can become disciplined enough to use it. Once you have mastered this art, you can, quite literally, 'make' someone talk. Ask a question, and when they have given as much of an answer as they feel is necessary, you simply say nothing in return. Pause for a moment longer than is comfortable and they will give you more – guaranteed.

Remember: the more the other person is speaking, the more they are opening their blind to let the communication flow. Even if the other person is quiet or shy; if you give them time and space to respond, they will open up. You could also practice subtle facial expressions as unspoken prompts or clues that you are expecting them to speak next.

- **Restatements:** This clever technique has two huge communication benefits. Firstly, it forces you to listen carefully, because you can't do it if you are not listening; and secondly, it shows the other person that you were listening carefully to what they were saying. Both these things build your credibility and open their blind. The idea is that you simply repeat back to them the same statement, without adding or subtracting a single word. This is another magician's trick that will compel the other person to expound on their original statement.

Person two: *"Well, I've been looking at several solutions to help sort this problem out."*

Person one (you): *"So, you've been looking at several options to help solve the problem."* (pause)

Person two: *"Yes, I've looked at A, but that has several issues, B, which seemed to work OK, and C, which is too expensive."*

Person one (you): *"too expensive?"* (pause)

Person two: *"Yes, we have a budget of around..."*

- **Comfortable probes:** Once you have started to open someone's blind, and only when that action is in process, you can begin to employ comfortable probes. Until you have a partially opened blind in front of you, obviously probing questions will come across as rude, irrelevant and uncomfortable. You need to work hard to get to this point, and you must deliver them well so that your customers will respond positively to you using appropriate, comfortable questions.

  "Would you tell me more about your evaluation process?" *"How will you decide whether to proceed?"* or *"What is the most important factor for you?"*

- **Sensitive probes:** At this point, the blinds on your communication partner's window are almost entirely open, and you can move into the arena of sensitive probing questions. If you have followed the steps laid out above, your listener will be so receptive to your communication that you can now ask sensitive questions. This is where you can delve deeper into the detail of their personal goals and motivations. The idea here is that it would be impossible to garner a positive response to these sort of questions, at the beginning of a conversation, because the other person's blind would be too closed.

"Would you expect to use a finance agreement to pay for this solution?" "What will finding a solution that works mean to you and your business?" or "What would be the impact of this in your day-to-day life?"

- **Interpretation:** Finally, after you have opened the communication blinds, won the other person's trust and gathered the information you need to be able to help them, you can start to format a solution. Before doing that, however, there is one last, vitally important stage to consider. You summarise the whole of the conversation in a simple statement. This proves you were listening, demonstrates that you understand and also indicates that you believe you have a solution for them. If you have executed this process well, they will be as interested in hearing from you as you have them up until this point.

"You have been looking at switching supplier for a while, but you were concerned that other systems might have similar issues as your current one and would be too expensive to install?"

The subtle shift from communication to selling

You will notice that the skills I have outlined so far in this chapter form a sales conversation. That is because there is very little difference between good communication and persuasive selling. In fact, in many instances, they are exactly the same thing.

But, Procter and Gamble did teach me a powerful framework that sits alongside the blind opening skills I have outlined above, known as the Five-Step Persuasive Selling Format.

1. **Summarise the situation:** Having opened your prospects' communication blinds and learned about their requirements in detail, you are now in a position to summarise their situation. Their reaction to your statement should indicate if you are correct and if there is any interest in you presenting your solution. If either of these responses is negative, you simply return to the window opening techniques until you have better understood their position.

2. **State the idea:** In the most simple, clear and concise language possible, tell your listener how your solution will work. Do not go into some great sales spiel – simply tell them how it meets the objectives they shared with you earlier, what the additional benefits will be, and how much it will make their life easier. My advice is to have the skeleton of this presentation rehearsed and practised beforehand, so you only need to tweak it accordingly for each prospect.

3. **Explain how it works:** Once again, the response will indicate whether you can proceed and get into the detail, or if you need to go back and firm up any previous conversation points. This stage is not a monologue or presentation; it is a further engagement to ensure that any objections are heard and overcome, any implementation details or delivery times are given, and the customer fully understands what is on offer.

4. **Reinforce the key benefits:** In stage two you presented the first draft of the idea, confirming the details and adjusting it accordingly. Now you need to benefits: ideally using the language that the prospect has used during the initial discovery conversation.

5. **Suggest an easy next step:** This is another way of saying that you ask for the order. If you have done the hard work up to now, this should be an 'easy' next step – but the truth is that most salespeople still struggle to close. Don't fear this – simply ask for the business – as they will never be more ready to say yes.

Translating face-to-face sales into online automation

Of course, this was a face-to-face selling technique that I learned over thirty years ago, long before the internet, social media and automated online sales had been invented. But

I wanted to share this technique with you because nothing has changed.

Yes, I mean it, not a single thing has changed in the psychology of selling.

- People still buy from people they trust
- They still buy from people who understand their needs the most
- And they still buy from the people who prove that they have listened by responding to their exact needs

And you can apply all of the skills I have explained above to automated online sales circuits. You can target adverts to the right people, personalise emails to capture highly targeted attentions, collect specific data, personalise responses, build rapport and trust, deliver relevant value, present information and close deals.

CHAPTER 7:

LEAD GENERATION
Irresistible treats for a hungry crowd

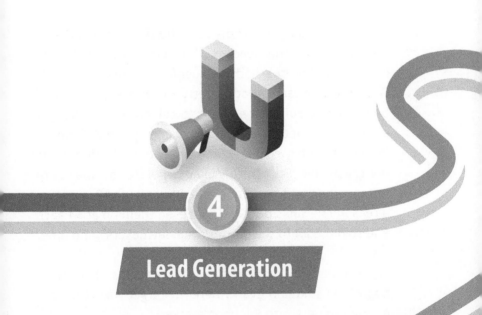

4

Lead Generation

Selling is easy: you just need to find a hungry crowd. You could attend every sales course in the world, learn how to sell ice to Eskimos and sand to Arabians, perfect your smoothest patter or pay a fortune for a Colgate smile: but none of that is necessary. You just need to locate people who want what you have got.

Back in 1990, when I arrived in Sydney from Brisbane, I decided it was time to invest in some transport of my own. I headed off to Kings Cross, the second-hand car dealing epicentre of the city and started looking around. It was about then that I realised cash flow might be an issue. I was juggling savings and credit card limits to best effect, but it had hit a bottleneck, and I needed cash fast. So, I decided to look for a quick fix.

While on holiday in Europe, I'd noticed an abundance of food sellers on the beaches. But here, on Bondi Beach, it seemed the idea hadn't caught on. I knew Australia Day was approaching and pretty much everyone would be heading down to the beach to celebrate. So, I bought a load of baguettes, salad, and fillings; packed them up nicely into a big cool box and headed off to find some hungry people. Each freshly filled baguette cost me 57c to put together, and my flatmate had suggested $2 would be a reasonable sales price. So, I labelled them up at $4 each and sold the lot to the patriotic holidaymakers in no time.

What I hadn't counted on, was requests. For every baguette I sold and even where my target wasn't hungry enough to part with $4, people asked for drinks. So, with a now-empty cool box, I walked about a kilometre to the nearest store and negotiated a bulk buy from the chiller cabinet. The RRP was $1.80 each, I paid the shopkeeper

$1.10 and loaded my cooler with cans: it fitted 33 exactly. Four trips later, selling them at $2 per can and (together with the baguette money) I had made about $500 for four hours work.

As I said, selling is easy. If you can find a market or an opportunity and you are prepared to work hard – you can always make money.

Market, message, media

In an earlier chapter about the four-step sales process, I described the first step as being qualification. Before you can enter that stage, however, you need to generate some leads. There is a degree of qualification that takes place at this point too, but it is not as detailed as the process I described earlier.

Your leads should include everyone and anyone who could potentially purchase from you. So, going back to the example I used then, about selling scuba dives on the beach, pretty much everyone there could be a potential lead. Yes, you will want to identify and capture information on the ones who want to buy now – but you should not ignore the ones who have the potential to move into that space at a future date.

The market, message, media principle can be applied at various stages of the lead generation and sales circuits: but the important thing is that it must be followed in this exact order. You cannot create a strong message before you have identified your market, and you cannot maximise the effect of any media until you have crafted the right message.

- **Market:** Before writing even one word of marketing copy, designing one social media advert, or even picking up the phone to make cold calls, you need to identify your market. If you were selling air, then perhaps everyone on the planet might be a valid target market – but even then, you'd be selling them something they can access for free. A smarter approach would be to repackage your product in a condensed format and sell it into the medical sector for ventilators or to scuba diving suppliers.

  Having a clear idea of exactly who will want to buy your goods and services is crucial to how easy it will be to sell to them. You need to locate and identify your hungry crowd. And the more accurate you can be in working out who they are, the more effective your marketing will be. We call these identities things like customer 'avatars' or 'personas' and try to bring them to life as a real person as much as possible.

- **Message:** With a finely tuned market avatar in your sights, you can now start crafting marketing that is explicitly directed at that person. Think about the headlines that will attract their attention, the stories they will identify with and warm to, and the value you can offer that will pique their interest. Then write to them in a way they will understand. If your target market works in the sciences you might like to share facts and statistics, if they are in entertainment, a little-hearted approach will attract, and businesses will be keen to save money or increase profits.

(These are generalist comments, and you should look at your avatar as a unique case.)

The more specific and targeted you can be with your message, the more effective it will be. And you should resist the default position of most sales communications in adopting a broad-brush approach. Marketing studies show time and time again that a refined message with a small target in mind will generate higher responses in that section of your lead base and still generate interest from the fringes and further afield.

- **Media:** The great thing about following the market, message, media approach to formulating your lead generation and sales communications is that the work can be repurposed. Once you have identified your market and crafted a message specifically for them, you can start experimenting across various types of media.

To start with, you might need to adopt a best-guess approach. For example, young people spend a lot of time on Instagram, while grandparents keep up with their family's activities on Facebook. The entrepreneur and small businesses communities favour LinkedIn as a social media platform, and Twitter seems to hover between them all. There are no hard and fast rules when it comes to the best social media platform in any given sector, but your experience will provide you with some clues, and you simply need to test and refine your activity.

Social media is often a long way from being the best media. There are many audience-specific exhibitions and tradeshows that put hundreds of specific prospects in the same venue as you. For example, engineers read engineering journals and local business owners attend networking events. You need to select the media that puts you in front of the specific avatar you have defined.

Multiple markets are better than one:

One of the things I hear all the time from business owners is that their business is different, and they don't have just one type of customer. I understand that: but their businesses are not different because of that. The companies that are different are the ones that do only have one type of customer – those would be very rare indeed.

All companies sell to a wide scope of customers, but their sales efforts will still be far more effective if they focus on one. Well one at a time to be more exact. If you want to maximise your sales, you need to get comfortable with complexity and segmenting your client base as much as you can. Look at your existing client base and identify the top twenty percent. Could you make them into one avatar, or even two, using the rules that I outlined above? Think how powerful that could be for your lead generation if you could create marketing and lead magnets directed specifically for companies like that.

Then break the next forty percent into another one or two avatars and so on. Once you have done this exercise once and created your campaign, you will find that it only needs slight tweaks to make it applicable to other categories. Do this well, and before you know it, you will have multiple streams of leads flowing into your funnels.

CHAPTER 8:

THE MILLENNIUM BUG

How we all bought into a 1000-year fear

As you start this chapter, you may well be asking what the millennium bug fiasco has to do with automated marketing or lead generation. Some readers might even be wondering what the millennium bug is, or was, and may never have heard the term before now. It is incredible how quickly the whole world forgets something that, for a time, consumed its fears, concerns and actions completely.

You could amuse yourself by Googling this piece of recent, and embarrassingly unimpactful, digital history. But, to save you the trouble, here is a brief overview of the millennium bug (also known as the Year 2000 problem, the Y2K problem, the Y2K bug, the Y2K glitch, or just Y2K).

Computers, as we know them today, were just beginning to be introduced to homes and workplaces in the late 1980s and early 1990s. Data storage was costly, so the developers tried to save space everywhere and only coded for the last two digitals of the year field (1986 was 86 and 1993 was 93). It was almost as if no one believed we would ever reach the year 2000 and have to deal with the distant future. As an aside, when you look at predictive films such as 2001: A Space Odyssey, Mad Max and Blade Runner, it is no wonder we thought the very idea of ever getting beyond the 1900s was preposterous.

In simple terms, the practice meant that the majority of the world's computers, which by 1999 had spawned to ubiquity, could not distinguish between the year 2000 and the year 1900. The general belief, even among the most tech-savvy people on the planet, was that this date glitch might just cause the world to stop turning on its axis. The result was a global question mark that no one seemed to know the answer to.

Information creates needs

I was working for Kraft in the lead up to 2000, helping to develop Systems Applications and Products (SAP) in readiness for Y2K. And I can tell you that they were not taking the task at hand lightly. Around the world, work started on a cure in October 1995; and it is estimated that by the time the new millennium dawned, more than a billion lines of customer code had been written and updated to save the digital catastrophe from occurring.

Then, as the fireworks filled the air and billions of champagne glasses clunked to mark the beginning of the 21st Century – nothing happened. For five years, behind the scenes in digital-land people had whispered in varying tones of mild or major concern. From the beginning of 1999, the media's rumour mill had hypothesised, prophesied and worked the rest of the world into a frenzy of terror at nobody knew quite what. And nothing happened – nothing at all. Within a week, people were still saying, *"can you believe it's the year 2000?"* but they had all forgotten about the dread of the millennium bug.

I then left Kraft in 2000 and moved to IBM where I worked with customers who had not finish implementing SAP in their organisation and still had many millions of pounds to spend on doing so.

*As a caveat, and out of respect for my former colleagues at Kraft and IBM (and all the other brilliant IT professionals of the day), it may be that their exceptional work solved the problem. The truth is that we will never know. There is every possibility that it was the greatest save that the digital world will ever witness. But history will forever record Y2K as a phenomenally expensive non-event where 'nothing happened'.

The reason for telling you the story is because it illustrates an incredible phenomenon about human attention. We will react to invisible things, en masse, if there are enough emotion and publicity created around them. Everyone actioned the millennium bug updates – everyone. Companies spent whatever it took to get their systems verified and as ready as they possibly could be for the predicted crash. Every digital file on earth was backed-up in preparation. Even people who didn't even know what backed-up meant had been gently cajoled into taking action.

Information highlights needs

There are many other examples of enormous markets being created out of nothing. Sticking with the digital world, it is only because of innovations from companies like Microsoft and Apple that we all have personal computers, smartphones and tablets today. Before they created the idea it was possible that everyone could own what IBM used to represent, we didn't even realise that we couldn't live without those things. They created needs and desires in the same way that Y2K generated the fear of the unknown.

I'm not suggesting that you have to do that in your business to generate leads or find a hungry crowd: but you could do. And even if you didn't create 'something out of nothing', you could certainly do more to highlight existing needs. As it happens, I have an idea for creating a need that the population of the world doesn't realise that it has yet, and I am working on a plan to launch it. I'll tell you more about that at the end of this book – but for now, let's look at how you can use Y2K lessons and principles to attract more leads for your business.

Information feeds needs

In 2003, I set up the company that I run today – EXELA. To begin with, I operated as a kind of sales gun for hire. My experience with companies like Proctor and Gamble, Kraft and IBM stood me in a very good light with anyone looking to sell increase their sales. I had also learned that selling was a process, so I knew how to adapt it to pretty much anything. I would take the brief from my clients, recruit a sales team for each particular project, teach them what to do and how to do it, and set them on their way.

In 2006, I bought a CRM product called Infusionsoft to help manage my own business and the projects I was taking on for my clients. It was amazing, and the more I learned about the automation capabilities of this new product, the clearer I began to see the opportunity for a new era of sales. Yes, CRM systems had been around long before that, in one form or another, but I had seen nothing quite like this level of engagement.

With my knowledge of the sales process finally being supported by software that could manage and support the intricacies of the process, our sales results were flying. I was so impressed that, as a famous advert of the 1990s would often state, I bought the company. Well, I didn't buy it, as such. In 2009 I became a reseller of Infusionsoft in the UK.

Today, we have worked with around 4500 Infusionsoft users and helped them to develop and fine-tune automated sales processes that get results. And all from a solution that, until fifteen years ago, was not available in the UK. In fact, not one of those 4500 clients even knew they needed the system that has launched, grown or kept their business alive, before that time.

People do not know what they don't know – and neither do the customers that your business has not converted yet.

Your job is to create the need and communicate it to the right market. Whether you have a product that solves a global problem that may or may not even exist or a service that helps companies treat each individual lead like the most important client on earth – you have to communicate the message.

CHAPTER 9:

LONG TERM NURTURE
Why online relationships lead to sales

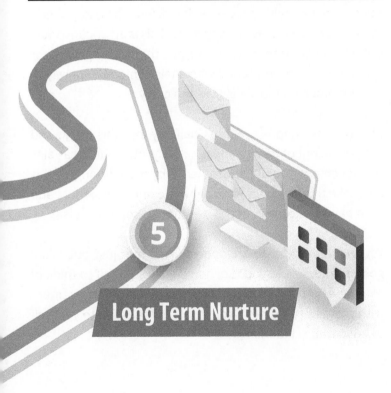

I have already made it clear that I believe selling is a process that can be learned and not a dark art that only some people possess the gift of. If there is one area of that process, however, that needs a level of skill and deep understanding of people, it is nurturing your audience and growing their confidence in what you do. Again, this can be learned; but it is a skill, and if you can find someone to help who is already good at this sort of thing, I would recommend doing that.

In the sales and marketing circuit that I talk about in this book, long-term nurture comes after you have generated the lead, made an offer and produced some action from your prospect – maybe even made your first sale. So, there is already a level of engagement. But here is where most salespeople or sales processes fall down. They stop there, thinking that the job is already done. This is an unconscious, but very deliberate, decision to put the responsibility for spending any more money with their company entirely in the customer's hands. It is lazy and crazy.

We are nine chapters, almost halfway into this book: and the equivalent of being almost halfway into building a sales relationship with your customer. Why would you get this far, make this much effort to generate one transaction, and then hand the control of the situation to someone else?

You wouldn't refer to anyone you had met just once as a good friend, would you? So, don't allow yourself to think of someone who has made one purchase or one engagement with you as a customer – you owe it to them and to yourself to build that relationship.

Nothing has changed: people still buy people (online or offline)

I talked in chapter three about the difference between marketing and sales. Well, at this stage of the circuit, you are still really on the cusp of the marketing process – even if a first small purchase has been made. To save you looking back, here is my general definition again:

"The role of marketing is to identify and collect leads by sharing information and creating an interest in the products and services that a company has to sell. The sales part of the process attempts to convert those interested leads into paying customers."

There are lots of practical techniques to help do this, but engagement (getting a response) and giving value are the underlying principles to follow. I'll give you a few ideas to try at the end of this chapter. But for now, I want to dig into the psychology of nurturing.

The phrase 'people buy people' is so well-known and universally spoken that its origin has long been forgotten. But its meaning is often missed too. People buy from people they trust. It is easy to see why you would trust someone you have known for a long time and whose character you can, to a certain extent, predict and rely on. Equally, you will know people who, based on the same criteria, you have decided you do not trust and would not place too much faith in. But these are people you know, face-to-face in the real world. What about a company who you are considering buying from online?

Online reputations come from three places. There are the reputations generated from what you already know about that company offline. For example, John Lewis's eCommerce website did not need to build a new brand when it launched in 1999 – the company was already known, loved and trusted by those who visited its stores. Then there are the reputations you form based on your own experiences and interactions. And finally, there are the stories, reviews and recommendations from anyone else who has shared a view online.

I will address the third one of those in chapters thirteen and fourteen, the first one is another story altogether, but the second one is the result of long term nurture. Reputation is everything in business. It determines how easy it is to attract customers, sell to customers, build loyalty and launch new things. For those reasons alone, it is worth the effort to nurture your prospects and continue to do so throughout the lifetime of that relationship.

Stories and substance

The single best way to relay any information is to turn it into a story. People remember stories more than a list of facts, they find stories more engaging and interesting than strings of data, and they will retell stories far more often than descriptions of products. So, wherever possible, when you are attempting to engage with your customers and prospects, tell them stories. And make the stories that you tell relevant, valuable and about the people whose trust you want to build.

People also want to feel like they received something of value from their engagement with your brand or business. They have asked for information (clicked the button), received an answer (your quote), and now it is up to you to persuade them that they are in the right place. Think carefully about the things that you can share, the value that you can give, questions you can ask or answer and the impression that you can leave by what you do next.

As I have said numerous times already, selling is a process, and you are deep into that process at this point. You are at a critical stage that will determine if your hard work will be worth the effort. Think hard, get creative and start to nurture those relationships.

Examples of nurture tools and techniques

- **Quizzes and questionnaires:** Offer your prospects the chance to rate their financial knowledge. Then ask them a series of relevant questions to assess where they are in relation to the rest of their market. This might generate a report which you can send them with an invitation to book a call and talk it through with an expert.

- **Blog posts:** Whenever you publish relevant content online, you increase the chances of Google sending the right people to your website. A good way to plan and drive the type of content you should publish (blogs, articles, videos, etc.) is to think about how you engage with prospects. Create content that has value and will impact lives. Tell people how to do things, educate them about the market, not just your stuff. Give away some of your best-kept expertise – help them decide to trust you.

- **Calculators:** People like to know what general information means to them personally. A great way to translate standard data into a useful and action-generating fact for a prospect is to give them a calculator. Then simply enter their own data, and your algorithm tells them what it means in real terms. You can issue the results to them there and then in real-time, or send it in a bespoke report that they have to download by sharing a bit more information. With a bit of thought, the possibilities are endless.

- **Resources:** As an expert in your sector, you should have a library of resources and information close to hand. This may be already written (technical sheets, technical instructions, coaching programmes, etc.) or tucked away in the minds of your longest-standing employees. Gather it together in sharable formats and make it available as resources that interested prospects can access, download or apply for.

With all of these things, you are simply exchanging value for information and engagement: so you can learn about your prospects, and they can see that you are involved and know what they want. You cannot have enough nurturing content, so put aside time to regularly create more, repurpose what you have and build it into your nurturing automation.

Nurture also means knowledge

All of these activities will increase your knowledge of individual clients and allow you to segment your database accordingly. As mentioned earlier, the tighter your understanding of your target market (or avatar), the more powerful your messaging can become. For example, your nurturing and engagement might reveal the headcount of various companies on your lists, so you will then know which ones to pitch your multi-user solutions to.

With a sophisticated sales automation system, like Infusionsoft, you can send prospects into various versions of your sales pipeline, depending on the actions and responses from the information that you send out.

CHAPTER 10:

HOW TO KRAFT A GREAT MESSAGE

Why marketing is a kind of project management

I mentioned previously that in 1993, as my wanderlust finally abated and I was settling into married life with Jacqueline, I landed a job at Kraft Foods in Cheltenham. It was a sweet appointment, as an Account Manager in the chocolate division, formerly part of Jacob Suchard. My roles evolved and changed, and eventually, I ended up in the private label part of the business, looking after accounts such as William Morrisons, Fortnum and Masons and Marks and Spencer.

Although still seen as a sales function, this was much more of a collaborative approach to sales than anything I'd known before, and it taught me a great deal about sales. Having spent three years selling one-off diving experiences to tourists on sunny beaches, I was now developing long-term taste experiences for major corporations. And yet, it was still all about building relationships through a process.

Sales and marketing is project management

Older readers who frequented Marks and Spencer will be familiar with their St Michael brand, which I believe was discontinued in the early 2000s. As with all of their products and lines they had to reflect a premium brand and St Michael confectionary was no different. So my role was to ensure that Kraft designed and developed a range of chocolate and other sweet things that met the standard and supported the brand. It was sales disguised as project management.

The first step was to engage with the buyers (they called themselves selectors) and understand the brand. This is the equivalent to the 'identifying your market' stage of any sales process that we covered in chapter seven. Then we had to develop the product, ensuring that the flavours and colours were inline with the client's expectation. Again, there is a similarity here with 'delivering the message' from the sales process. And finally, we were involved in developing the brand, packaging and marketing messages that would help our client sell more product from the shelves.

As the seller, we were doing all the proactive questioning and information gathering. We built a process to deliver the result, and we were responsible for keeping the communication lines open and growing a close relationship with our customer. The operational aspects of the sale were different from anything I had done before, and yet the principles were fundamentally the same.

So, what working at Kraft taught me was that really, sales is just project management. It was also an example of long-term nurture because developing products was a lengthy process and meant paying close attention at every stage.

Big nappies and persistence

The other type of long term nurture in sales is none other than persistence. Sometimes you just have to keep plugging away until your prospect or customer gives in and says yes. We have all heard the stories about authors such as Stephen King and John Grisham getting dozens of rejection letters before finally being recognised. I think JK Rowling received twelve such replies before getting the bestselling book of all time published. There is a lot to be said for persistence.

But the secret sauce that gives persistence a little more kick is relationships. If you get to know your prospect or customer and you nurture that relationship, then you are many times more likely to sell to them at some point in time than simply by knocking on the door.

One of my Proctor and Gamble clients was Asda, way back in the late 1980s when they were running large stores rather than supermarkets. They were still a sizeable customer, however, and I had built up a good relationship with one of their buyers – a guy called Mark Chamberlain.

One of the lines at the time was Pampers Nappies: but not the compact and convenient product that mums and babies are privileged to buy today. These nappies were massive, and the value pack was a shelf-breaker. I hasten to add that

I wasn't involved in the product development for Pampers; but whoever was hadn't thought it through very well. The nappy was basically just wadding, rather than the super absorbent, lightweight and minimalist materials that had since been developed. And to add insult to injury, vacuum shrink-wrapping wasn't really a thing back then either, so the value pack resembled a bale of hay.

None of the supermarkets or independents liked them as they could only fit three or four on a shelf, and as soon as they sold, it left an unattractive gap. But it was on my list of products, so every time I visited Mark in the Asda Head Office on Great Wilson Street in Leeds, I would mention nappies. It almost became a game between us, and I would spend my journey there trying to come up with a new clever analogy or hidden benefit to being the only major retailer in the UK selling Pampers value packs. But he wasn't budging and resisted all my efforts.

Then, one day, I was in our office at Harrogate, and I got a call from the customer service department querying an order. Someone from Asda had just asked for three lorry loads of Pampers value packs to be delivered, and the girl who took the order was convinced it had been a mistake. No one had ever done that before.

So, I called Mark and could almost feel his self-amused smile down the line as he confirmed that I had finally worn him down and he was prepared to give them another try. Shortly after that, the product was relaunched in a format more akin to what mums and dads buy today. But the day that order came in will always count as one of my most satisfying wins.

How to craft an engaging message

There is one more thing that I need to mention in this chapter. And it is about engagement through storytelling. You see, project management, sales circuits, long-term nurture and any other customer relationship building process is really about telling the story. And to tell a story well, you need to know its purpose.

In the world of fictional, made -up stories, there are two types of storyteller. The ones who have an intricate plot laid out before they even start writing and those who invent characters and situations then put pen to paper and see where the story takes them. But in the non-fiction, real-world, life just happens as it happens: there may be a plan, but there is no pre-determined plot.

In a business setting, where storytelling is at the root of every relationship; you must use a mixture of the two approaches. You need to get to know the characters and their circumstances – today, in their version of the real-world – and you also need to have a clear idea of the plot (or where you want the story to go). The reality is that the story will rarely pan out in the way that you want or expect it to. But there are two important things to remember. Firstly, if you have a plan or a plot, you will be better able to steer the flow back on track or choose a different path. And secondly, as the salesperson (the author of the sales circuit) you should always be in control of the narrative.

Please don't take this section lightly and write-it off as fantasy. If you approach business as a story and take responsibility for being the one telling the story – you will be able to dictate the outcome of every situation more than you think.

CHAPTER 11:

CLIENT ONBOARDING

Create the sale that just keeps on giving

Client Onboarding

Wouldn't it be great if every time you won a hard-fought battle you knew there would be three or four easy ones to follow before the next challenge came along?

Anyone who has ever run a business, tried to sell anything, or dealt with customers on any level; will tell you that exchanging goods and services for revenue always presents problems – especially with new customers. Wherever expectation and delivery meet, there is the potential for friction. The buyer is expecting to receive the value that they have paid, and the seller is trying to deliver said value within the confines of the revenue they received. But these two, apparently equal, values are rarely perceived the same way.

Sink or swim?

In the sales automation circuit, we call the process of starting to deliver a new sale 'client onboarding'. The image is an important factor in turning every sale into a platform for perpetuating future business growth and scale. Picture a pleasure cruiser sailing across the sea of opportunity that is your 'entire target market' (where all your perfect clients live). On this fabulous craft are all the goods or services that you provide; along with luxury accommodation and well trained, polite and knowledgeable staff ready to wait on their every need. There are facilities galore, and if any request is beyond the existing capability of the crew, they simply create a solution out of thin air. A customer could travel the seven seas, and never find another vessel that even comes close to the service and splendour of this one.

You might think I am being a little over the top with my imagery here, but if you look at how 9 out of 10 small businesses describe themselves on their websites and other marketing, you'll see that I am not far wrong. Their promises will include: we give the best service, we are the industry experts, we are highly competitive, and (most ambitious of all) we really do care about our customers. The implication is that none of their competitors does these things – even though every single one of them makes the same promises. The problem is that on most of these company's boats, their existing clients are either hanging on for dear life or fighting to stay in the lifeboats that are tied to its edges.

Every time you win a new bit of business you have the opportunity to bring them safely onboard; treat them like royalty, give them a guided tour, settle them in and prove to them they have just made a decision they will never regret. Then, once they are safely on board; comfortable, satisfied and a converted advocate of your particular mode of transport, they'll be open to hearing about anything else you have to offer. More than that, though, they'll happily fly your flag and wear your colours whenever they visit the mainland or stop off at another port for a while.

I think you get the picture: so, I'll leave the nautical analogy there for the while and explain precisely how you successfully onboard a client using both automated and in-person techniques.

The three benefits of successful onboarding

There are three invaluable benefits to having a strong onboarding process. And these are critical, both in the first instance and as a part of the entire sales automation circuit.

1. Satisfied customers are likely to buy again, buy more things, and stay loyal to the supplier
2. Fulfilled customers are easier to look after, cost less time to manage and generate more profitable income
3. Happy customers say good things about their suppliers and (with encouragement) can generate referrals

Become a product of your planning

Take, for example, a company selling garden furniture. A new customer sets up an account after going through the various other stages described in this book, and their first order comes through the website. Most suppliers would simply rub their hands together, take the money and send the instruction to the warehouse in the hope that the stock arrives undamaged and they don't ask for a refund later.

But this company understands the importance of client onboarding. So, at the same time, the order makes its way to the warehouse an email is generated thanking the customer for their order and telling them exactly what will happen next. There might even be a picture of one of the warehouse staff, and the email could be addressed from them personally. The customer's new friend explains how they will locate the stock, pack it with recycled cardboard and biodegradable tape, and personally ensure it is loaded safely on the delivery vehicle.

They might even make a few suggestions about the best way to protect the furniture from the elements or share a favourite pancake recipe if they wanted to enjoy breakfast on their new table. The more personal and relevant to the purchase you can make this communication, the better. And don't worry, you do not need to write it from scratch every single time: all of the content can be prewritten, tweaked by product and automated.

Your most successful open rate ever

In email marketing, open rates are the holy grail. So, consider for a moment the open rate you can expect from the email a new customer receives within one minute of sending you their hard-earned money for the first time ever. Yes, that is right; 100 % is not an unreasonable expectation. They want to know that you have received payment, that you have acknowledged the order and that what they purchased is safely entering your delivery process.

While you have got their full attention, use it. Assure them that they have made a brilliant decision in buying from you. Manage their expectations by detailing the exact delivery information and how to get in touch or find answers. Think of ways to get them to read your blog by suggesting there is valuable information there. Tell them about the other products you sell (subtly and non-salesy, of course). And think of any other way you can to build the trust they have just decided to place in your company.

Other trust-building and reputation making ideas for your onboarding emails (you can send more than one) include:

- Videos of the product in action
- Updates if it is a bespoke product that needs building or has a longer delivery time
- Technical, environmental, or other relevant information (only share interesting things – don't bore them)
- Links to associated product pages (for cross-selling or upselling)
- Links to profiles of other staff involved in the delivery (friendly faces make all the difference)
- Personal messages from the owner of the business
- Invite them to join your customer membership site and access more free stuff

One great example of onboarding that I saw was from a car showroom. The customer had ordered a new Mini Cooper – it was a beautiful looking car with a convertible roof, and sports trim. They had clearly visited the showroom at a previous date, maybe several months before, and specified various colours, add-ons and personalised features. So, the salesperson, presumably the same one who had sold them the car, had put together a video on her mobile phone of the car coming into the showroom. She couldn't have been more enthusiastic as she skipped around the Mini, pointing out the personalised areas, demonstrating the sunroof and even showing off the purr of the engine. It was truly engaging.

The video was exciting to watch as a third-party onlooker, so just imagine being the recipient of this video and seeing the car that would be delivered to your door in a few days. Massive value that is guaranteed to be shared with dozens of friends (and even made its way to me) that cost just five minutes of the salesperson's time to make.

Service with a smile

Much of what I have described above is equally relevant to a company selling services, but here are a few additional ideas for onboarding if that is relevant to what you do.

Services, whether it is consultancy, training, support or advice, tend to require a bit of scheduling. Diaries need to be cross-referenced; rooms might need to be booked, and various other types of preparation or pre-work are often necessary. So, your initial onboarding communication is an ideal time to start demonstrating your professionalism, thoroughness, and clear communication style. Let your customer know the standard they can expect. Done well, a strong sequence of onboarding communications can turn a new customer into a raving fan long before you have even set foot in their office to deliver your services.

From professional services and coaches through to performing artists and tradespeople, the onboarding email can be one of your strongest USPs. That extra little bit of work can make a huge amount of difference.

Imagine you had just selected a firm of decorators to come and paint your house. Before they arrive to view the job and go through the details of what you need, this happens: A selection of colour swatches arrive in the post. An email pops into your inbox the same afternoon with the headline 'Welcome to your beautiful new interior' and links to the websites of the local paint suppliers. The email explains the pros and cons of each type of paint and gives helpful advice about the cost and application benefits of each one.

There are also links to pictures and case studies of other jobs that the firm have completed in your area recently and testimonials of all their delighted customers. And remember – this is all after you have already agreed to use them – all this is doing is making you feel fantastic that you have made such a smart choice. So, by the time they arrive at your house, you will already love them, have tea and biscuits ready for them and be fully confident that they are going to do a fabulous job.

Who else do you know?

I mentioned earlier that the third big benefit of successful customer onboarding is referrals: generating opportunities for them to pass on your details to others. Well, I will cover more about that fruitful part of the process in chapter fifteen, but for now, consider this the groundwork. Ask any gardener what the magic ingredient of growing is, and they will tell you that the soil (or foundation) that you choose makes a massive difference.

CHAPTER 12:

COUNTING THE COST OF WINNING VS LOSING

Why hard-fought victories can end in defeat

Do you know the old saying about winning the battle at the cost of losing the war? From a distance, it is an obvious strategy to avoid, and anyone can see there is no point in gaining a few small successes if you are going to lose out big time in the end. The driver who leads for 45 laps of a 50-lap race but crosses the line in 4th place will soon be forgotten. And while Windows will forever be associated with Microsoft, did you know it was first featured in the Xerox Alto – a personal computer launched in the 1970s. Being first, or gaining short-term wins is not always the same as an overall victory.

In some cases, it is actually the short-sighted attraction of chasing a quick win that actually causes the downfall of the campaign. Chess is a classic example of strategic sacrifice from one player being a route to them winning the game.

Known as gambits or traps, these are sequences of moves that give the semblance of retreat or loss but ultimately lead to positions of strength.

We have already spoken about making offers and giving away free information or discounts to gain a lead or a foot in the door with a potential new client. So, what I want to talk about in this chapter is the importance of having a strategy and seeing the bigger picture of an entire sales process – not just a one-off sale.

A circuit is a safe place to grow a business

Most processes are described in a straight line: even traditional sales theory when taught in most books and training courses take that format. The very fact that the sale ends with something called a 'close' highlights the limited view of the opportunity. My version of closing is the client onboarding and long-term nurturing topics I've described over the last few chapters – but they are clearly not the end of the story. For me, that is just the first stage of an ongoing (systematically repeating) journey towards long-lasting relationships. Quick wins are no way to build a business, and in many instances are a sure-fire way to kill it off completely.

Another version of this failing in many businesses is the inability to build on winning positions and strengthen an opportunity while being ahead of the game. Sometimes you need to take a step back, secure your position and take a strategic look at the surrounding area and the horizon. The best place to do this is while you are regularly winning business in the sales circuit, and everything is ticking over nicely. When you are under pressure, and the heat is on, you are more prone to rash judgements that are likely to bring calamity to your door. I say this because I know that a lot of business owners will sit back and chill out when they have just had a big win – revelling in their success and ignoring their flat spare tyre.

I'm not suggesting you shouldn't celebrate when you win—simply encouraging you not to rest on your laurels and forget the process that brought you to that place. The beauty of a repeating circuit is that you can measure, tweak and improve each time you go around. And client onboarding as a process is one step of that circuit, but also represents the bigger purpose of the circuit as a whole. It is managing the process to ensure the wheel keeps on turning ever more efficiently.

You can never win by playing games

Have you ever heard of an elite sportsperson who simply turns up on the day and wins the gold medal or a self-made billionaire who genuinely just got lucky? There are plenty of top performers in every field from entertainment to sport, and throughout the world of business who may make what they do 'look' easy – but believe me, it isn't. Behind every easy Hollywood smile, chauffeur-driven Rolls Royce and well-deserved luxury holiday lie years of blood, sweat and tears.

Although attributed to many people, the Gary Player version of the quote, "the more I practice, the luckier I get" makes so much sense. Golf is one of those games where, as an outsider, you can't help but think it is the luck of the bounce the run of the green or just sheer chance that makes a champion. Very similar is the multi-credited saying, "it took me twenty years to become an overnight success." Perhaps the very fact that the origin of these philosophies and observations are so difficult to pin down to one individual is testament to the deep truth behind them. Successful people everywhere are proud to make them their own because it gives a glimpse into what went into making the outward appearance. You can only become the best in whatever you do by being committed, paying attention to the details, following a tried tested and proven process and practising daily.

I have found this to be true throughout my life and business career, and the truth is that I am still getting there. For many of those early years, I didn't even know where I was going or why (just like my travel and scuba diving adventures), but I was watching, learning and applying myself to the task in hand at every turn. There are lessons in everything that we do, but most people don't stop long enough or observe close enough to turn a lesson into an improvement in the process.

As I've said in an earlier chapter, selling is easy – all you have to do is apply the process and keep adapting it until it works. Well, I believe that life is easy too. Of course, you are going to fail along the way, things are going to get tough from time to time, and there may even be a few knock out blows flying around. But the way to navigate it is the same as the way to design and implement a sales circuit. Strategically and on purpose.

And you can't do that if all you ever do is play at it or go in half-heartedly. If you are going to do something, you have to show proper interest in doing it well and getting it right. I am not pretending to be the best small business owner on the planet or even claiming to be a guru on selling and marketing. I don't own a Ferrari, live in a mansion, sail the Bahamas in my private yacht or go on holiday to exotic locations half a dozen times a year. But I do believe that I have applied myself to be the best I could be at everything that I have really cared for in my life. And that approach has built me a level of achievement, success and security that I am proud of and content with.

If you want to succeed in your business, you have got to take it seriously.

Get on board and get interested

A few years ago, after my father's partner passed away, he started to suffer from a little bit of dementia. It is perhaps a telling feature of human nature that when things like that happen to the people you love the most: you start paying attention. What I tried to do was encourage him to do more activities and get involved in various things; but his answer was mostly, "but I am not interested in that." Another feature of human nature, especially in emotive situations is that you self-evaluate a lot more. So, from that time, I decided that I would become more curious about a lot more things.

For example, I'd always had a passing interest in sport, but not what you would call a passion. Today, however, I could confidently engage in a conversation with an enthusiastic motor-racing or rugby fan – and not feel like a fraud in doing so. You have a choice in life. And and not just the way that you are born or influenced when growing up. It is a choice to be interested or not interested in anything. And the fact is that life is a lot more fun and fulfilling if you are interested in things. You'll find that you are more successful, more fulfilled and happier if you develop and invest in your curiosity gene.

Ask any child what their favourite subjects are at a school and then ask in which classes they get better grades: and you will get pretty much the same answer every single time. I'm not saying that you need to watch test cricket if you have better things to do with five days of your life or get into boxing if you are a pacifist. Nor do I expect people who would prefer to look on the bright side of life to develop a taste for politics, necessarily. We will all have some form of deep-set bias or taste in our psyche.

But if you want to get better at business, I encourage you to get interested in more things and make sure it is a curiosity-driven interest rather than a superficial one. If you want to bring new customers onboard, grow their trust in your ability to look after them and show them that choosing you was a good decision – get interested in them.

CHAPTER 13:

REVIEWS & TESTIMONIALS

Why one third-party word matters more than ten of your own

Review & Testimonials

In the social media age, reviews and testimonials have never been more important. Of course, getting independent feedback from other customers has always mattered. But it has never been more accessible than it is through online social channels, and it has never formed such a critical part of the buying process as it does today. I don't think that it is because we have, as a culture, become more cynical or careful – but simply because it is there.

Reviews and testimonials clearly matter in today's online buying environments. So why don't more companies, especially small businesses, make an effort to collect and manage them?

If you are looking to sell – it is always good to look from the perspective of the buyer. So, let's examine the way most people make purchasing decisions in the internet age. If you do things like this, so will your customers. Which means it would be a smart move to make it easier for them to choose you.

The modern buyer's decision-making process

1. **Search:** In the olden days, you had to do a lot of walking or driving around or reading articles to research the best option for what you were looking to buy. Or it may be that you had seen an advert on the TV or in a magazine, or one of your friends/colleagues had turned up with something new. Now, when people are looking for something, they simply

type a few keywords into Google (or another search engine) and see what is offered.

2. **Research:** Depending on what you are looking to buy (cost, size, purpose) either you will click on the first one that looks reasonable, or you will enter a period of research. This involves looking at various websites, comparing specifications, costs and availability. Eventually, you will arrive at two or three options that suit your criteria. Then you need to decide where you will spend your money.

3. **Reviews:** No longer is what a company claims about its products and services going to be enough. Savvy buyers want to know what other people's experience with a company and its products has been. They want to know first-hand if what the marketing says is true.

My research, my customer's experiences and my personal habits all tell me the same thing. We look at the number of reviews, feel fairly secure if the average rating is over four-stars out of five and read the first few reviews. People rarely read more than a handful of reviews and might go and check out a few outliers with only one star; but do you know – that is a good thing. If I arrived at a product with 347 five-star reviews and not a single negative, I think I'd be a little suspicious. Most people know that there are grumpy complainers out there with too much time on their hands or competitors with a grudge to bear.

The search engines themselves have their own reviews and scoring systems. Then there are the independent collators of reviews and recommendations, such as TripAdvisor for holidays, Checkatrade for tradespeople and Trust Pilot for everything else. The other thing to remember here (and this is why every business should make reviews a priority), is because Google loves them. If you have reviews on your website (the more and the higher the ratings, the better) or on third party sites pushing people towards your buying channels, Google (and most other search engines) will prioritise you and point more people your way.

Smart businesses also collect their own on their websites, social media sites, printed materials and waiting room walls. The benefit of this is that you can control how and when they are sent out or viewed, and you can influence what your customers say in them – to a certain extent.

Before I cover what makes a good review or testimonial, one last word of warning and encouragement. You must get them for your business. It doesn't matter if you don't work in a sector that traditionally relies on them (trades, products, etc.) you still need them. People will expect them, want to read them, be reassured by them and wonder why you haven't got them if they are missing.

Getting great reviews and ordering your own testimonials

Everyone is busy. So, the two essential things to remember when getting people to leave referrals are as follows.

Firstly, you need to ask people to do it. Trust me, no one (not even the best customer you have ever had or your biggest fan) will wake up tomorrow morning thinking, "I must go and write David at EXELA a review." So, you need to ask people to write them. And that leads me to the second point.

It is a big ask to expect someone to stop what they are doing and spend time and effort thinking about you. So, your job is to make putting pen to paper or fingers to keyboards on your behalf the simplest thing in the world for them to do. The best way to do this is to send them a link. See, I told you it was simple.

If there is a distinction between reviews and testimonials, then it is this. Reviews are a numbers game because potential buyers will look at how many there are and what the average star-rating is (even if they do go on to read a few of them in detail). Testimonials, on the other hand, are more of a personal reflection or statement about your business and the service you deliver.

Testimonials are also far easier for you to collate, manage and distribute. You could even write them for your customers or suggest the sort of things that they should say. Let me be clear here: I am not suggesting that you make up testimonials – that is a criminal offence and is way beneath any decent business owner. But, if you have had a conversation with a customer where they have said good things about you, and you get their permission to write that up as a testimonial – that counts. I would advise you send the written version back for sign off first – but that is a legitimate recommendation of your work in anyone's book.

Another great way to generate effective testimonials is to ask customers to write about a particular thing you did for them. Most people just ask for testimonials, but that is often too random or general to have a big impact.

The most powerful testimonials in the world

Here is a great exercise that will help you to gather a database of strategic and highly effective testimonials.

Start by making a list of all the objections that you regularly get to buying your products or services. Categorise them by type and then look among your current customers to see who 'used to think that' or who you feel can prove that is not an issue. Ask those customers if they are happy to answer a few questions, fill in a survey or write you a testimonial and then shape the conversation towards those issues. Be as specific as you can, and you could even explain why you are asking them if your relationship is strong enough. Remember, most people do want to help others. (You could even return the favour by sharing this technique with them for their business.)

Once you have your objection-overcoming testimonials, simply load them up on your sales pages, landing pages, social media pages and paid advertisements. It is the ultimate way of saying 'yes – we can help you' to a prospect who hasn't even asked you that question or raised the objection yet.

One last word on using powerful testimonials, before I move on to how I built my business one small step at a time.

Do you remember the last time that you were watching TV, and someone mentioned the place you were born, or they had the same surname as you? What effect did it have on you? I remember when I was travelling and selling scuba diving excursions to holidaymakers, I knew I was onto a winner if they were English. People love connections, and they will give that extra layer of trust to someone they feel an affinity or kinship with.

So, if you are marketing to accountants, send them testimonials from an accountant you already work with. If you are targeting sports associations, send them testimonials from other organisations you help with a sports connection. And so on. Strategic testimonials are powerful tools within the sales circuit, but most companies either ignore them or use them without any plan or purpose.

CHAPTER 14:

HOW I BUILT EXELA

One small step and one reliable system at a time

After helping to save the world from millennium bug meltdown in 2000, I worked for IBM for a couple of years, selling Systems Applications and Products (SAP), before joining an Oracle reseller business. I then decided the time had come to set up my own business and taking charge of the circuit for myself.

Looking back at my travelling and working history; it does now seem apparent that I was always one of those people who felt more settled when I was calling the shots. If I'm honest, I was probably the wrong fit for the corporate world – too much of a 'do it my way' type of attitude. So, I launched EXELA in 2003 as a sales agency where I would recruit, train and manage sales teams for my clients; either for short term projects or until they were able to manage themselves. But I had always been attracted to technology and found that I had an aptitude for understanding it and spotting applications for it. And the more I used technology within business the more I felt drawn towards the process side of sales rather than the natural flair that only a few seemed to possess.

After discovering the benefits of Infusionsoft in 2006 and using it in my business and for my customers for three years, in 2009 I became a reseller and set the course for the future of EXELA to date. The focus of the business became selling and supporting clients to build their businesses. This meant creating automated sales circuits, lead generation and conversion, marketing systems, customer service and sales management. And we became very good at what we do.

Award-winning simplicity

At the time of writing, my company has worked with over 4500 Infusionsoft customers. We are the only company to have consistently been ranked inside the top ten resellers of Infusionsoft, worldwide, since 2009: and most of those years within the top five. To be clear here, this wasn't because we sold more. Infusionsoft was sending us customers at the time, so we set up a process for managing lots and lots of set-ups and servicing contracts. Whether it is sales, service, production or management – you can only cope with volume if you have a robust process.

But here is the thing. We just do simple stuff. In essence, we practice what we preach and generate a lot of interest. Then we convert a lot of it into orders and look after our customers extremely well. There are bigger resellers out there than EXELA, especially in the USA where the product lives and is developed, and there are more glamorous ones who come top of the tree from time to time. But no one is more consistent than us: and I don't think there is anyone who creates more individual orders year-on-year than we do. The bigger companies tend to do the really fancy stuff and make the system dance like Fred and Ginger. We are the equivalent of a Ford production line, delivering one result after another in any colour you like as long as it works.

The reason for telling you this is not to brag or sell you an Infusion soft system from EXELA, but to demonstrate that you don't have to be flash to be good at sales and you don't need the gift of the gab to close a deal. You simply need to understand that sales is a process, and once you have got it right, you can press the button and watch it deliver. Of course, as with any system, it will need maintenance and tweaking to improve performance now and then – but essentially it will look after that side of the business.

Then I got the sack

And, as I mentioned earlier, this doesn't just apply to sales. I'd attended an Infusionsoft Partner Conference in November 2013 and something triggered in my mind. If I was going to grow this business properly, I needed to be free from the doing. So, I gave myself three months' notice that my services would no longer be required in the business. Seriously, it was an official written document that barred me from doing any of the work that I was currently doing. I had, in effect, given myself the sack.

So, by January of 2014, I'd employed Jamie and taught him everything I knew, supported by the simple processes and systems I'd set up. Six months later, Andrew joined the business, and I'd replicated myself again.

Sales as a process sets your brilliance free

If you are reading this book because you have chosen sales as a career and want to improve, I hope you have gleaned some value from my experiences so far. If that is you, I would encourage you to revisit and study chapters five and six again about the sales process and my time at Proctor and Gamble learning persuasive selling and communication skills. And I'd hope that you gain some insights into the importance of client onboarding and nurturing customers from those chapters. But I suspect you are reading this book because you recognise that you don't have a business without sales but acknowledge that sales are not really your thing.

You are probably brilliant at what you do and build amazing products or provide outstanding services. It may be that your competitors can't touch you for quality and your unique selling points are market beaters. But, what is the good in being the best in class if no one knows that you exist or your second-grade competitors are first-class at marketing?

There is no doubt that Lionel Messi is the best football player of his generation (maybe a handful of Ronaldo fans might argue the case – but go with me on this for now). But he would not have scored as many goals as he has, won as many awards and become a legend in his own lifetime if it hadn't been for his teammates. The industry, vision and consistency of players like Xavi and Iniesta are major contributors to Messi's genius.

Lewis Hamilton will go down in history as one of the greatest racing drivers of all time – his record speaks for itself. I would not want to undermine or take away one ounce of credit from his remarkable achievements. When someone, quite literally, puts their life on the line every day they go to work – they are worthy of their success. But surely the cleverest manoeuvre he ever made was his switch from McLaren to Mercedes in 2013. I wonder what the story would have been if he hadn't found the reliability and consistency of car to back up his talent.

Can you think of any big-name, mega-star actor who hasn't got at least one or two shockers attributed to their name? I certainly can't. Kevin Costner's costly flop, Waterworld springs to mind, along with George Clooney suffering a thud in Batman and Robin, and Cate Blanchett really missed the target in a forgettable adaptation of Robin Hood. Even the great Daniel Day-Lewis himself scored a less than perfect performance in the 2009 film, Nine. One film critic for that movie wrote, "How can a movie starring six Academy Award-winning actors be such a bore?"

You see, even the best in the business need a great script, system, team or process behind them to bring out their greatness. And you are no different in your business. I have no doubt that you are good at what you do. And you owe it to yourself to make sure you find a great way to build a sales system that can tell the world.

Building one day at a time with an eye on the future

Once I had relinquished my duties as the primary 'doer' in the business, I was free to explore the selling and building the business side of being an entrepreneur. (It wasn't until then that I even realised that is what I had become.)

Over the next few years, I created ways to bring in my own new customers on a low-cost onboarding engine. Instead of the industry-standard £2000 kickstart, I could offer people an automated version for £200. Then, around about 2016, I started workshops and courses to teach people in a classroom setting. Once EXELA became the go-to training, project and support company, sales just kept coming in. The thing to remember here is that software is a subscription model, and every single customer I have pays my business a monthly retainer. I'll let you think about the numbers from what I mentioned earlier, but suffice to say that a strong process-driven business model gives you freedom and flexibility on a massive scale.

In 2019, Infusionsoft changed its name to Keap, and we began selling their new CRM solution – a seamless transition for our business simply because of the processes that we have put in place. And within the first year, we are already ranking as one of the top performers worldwide.

As I said before, we practice what we preach and do exactly what we teach our customers to do. I have an accountant who looks after the numbers, and I use Xero (cloud accounting software) to manage transactions, reports and forecasting.

Yes, I could do my own accounting and have quite a good understanding of those things, but why would I want to? My time, focus and expertise are far more valuable to my business when I focus on what I am the expert at doing. I have administration staff on my team who look after all those daily tasks that have to get done. My marketing team focus on branding, messaging and communicating news with our customers. And the technically brilliant people in my business make sure everything works the way it should for our customers and us.

This leaves me to focus on the job of building the business one day at a time. I spend time looking at the circuit, measuring results, trying new things, tweaking and testing and dreaming of space. Yes, you did read that last word correctly. I spend time thinking about space, the future, and the possibilities and opportunities of being an entrepreneur in the 2020s. My vision of the next fifty years, with me in it (and I am already several years over fifty) include; developing the idea of space exploration, pushing the boundaries of technology, setting the scene for the next great leap of humankind and being curious about everything.

I know that I can only do that one day at a time, but I need to make the most of each of those days. I also know that it is the process I have worked hard to build into my business that allows me the freedom to pursue that dream. And I will tell you a more about my growing obsession with space in chapter 18.

THE SALES CIRCUIT | DAVID HOLLAND

CHAPTER 15:

REFERRALS

How to triple every sale without even trying

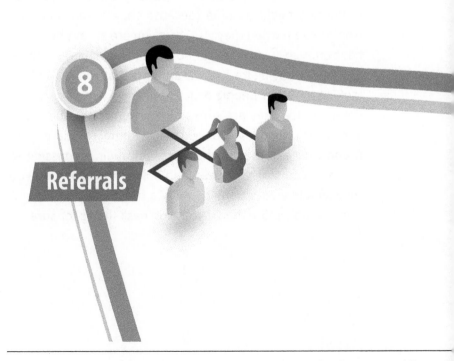

Referrals

The number of companies that don't ask for referrals will never cease to amaze me. When you lay out the psychology, effectiveness and ease of asking for referrals – like I am going to in this chapter – it amounts to nothing short of craziness that every company doesn't do it regularly.

The only easier way of generating sales through a referral scheme is asking for repeat orders from satisfied customers. And there is no better way of getting new business than asking satisfied customers who else they know who are similar to them. All you have to do is ask – it is that easy.

You see, the problem is that most of your customers (especially if you sell to consumers rather than other businesses) don't even consider that you are looking for new business. They don't think like a business, they think like people who want what you sell, so it is up to you to tell them.

If you run a dental practice or opticians, for example, your customers might assume (because they spend time in a waiting room when they visit) that you are always busy and have enough customers already. But if you explain to them as they are paying for their treatments that you are, in fact, looking for other people exactly like them, who appreciate great service, they are sure to know someone. And if you add a little incentive to encourage them to share their friend's details, they might even seek their permission to do so. If you serve 50 people in a day, how many do you think would give you the name of a friend – just like them? Considerably more than if you didn't ask that is for sure.

The best leads that you could possibly get

And here is the other brilliant thing about referrals. The person who knocks on your door because someone who they already know, like and trust has recommended you doesn't need that much convincing to buy. These sort of leads are gold dust – and yet most businesses never ask for them.

These are the foundation stones of an effective referral generating system:

1. **Great service:** You cannot build a steady stream of referrals if you are not worthy of being referred – it just will not happen. The biggest resistance anybody has to the idea of recommending goods and services to people they know is the possibility that it might dent their own reputation. Nobody wants to be on the end of that conversation.

   But if you give outstanding service, head and shoulders above anything that your competition puts out there, your customers will be more than happy to share the news. In fact, their motivation will be the exact opposite to their fear – they will love the idea of being the person who helps their friend get a better deal.

   So, if you genuinely do give an excellent service, you simply have to find a way of bringing a stream of referrals into your business. It would be nothing short of criminal to ignore this part of the sales circuit. The truth is that if you are the best thing since sliced bread, people will recommend you anyway. But, even if that is the case, you should still add in extra motivation to increase the activity.

2. **Incentivise sharing:** Even your biggest fans need a little encouragement. After all, we live busy lives, and no one wakes up in the morning, thinking "I wonder how I can help David find more Keap or Infusionsoft customers?" But despite our busy lives, it is also built into human nature to help the people we know, like and trust if we can. And all it takes is a reminder and a little encouragement.

The first and most basic step is simply to ask your existing customers if they will help by recommending you to other people they know. People like themselves who appreciate the great service they receive from you and your company. After that, you can come up with a range of fun, inventive and referral generating schemes and offers to encourage people to share your name with their friends.

Offers that work well include things like:

- a 50% off voucher for each referral who becomes a customer
- a free service for every three referrals
- an upgrade to the premium service for a year when your friend joins on the basic level
- or a copy of your new book after each referral's first order

Obviously, the type of business and the value of your products impact the offer you create, but all it needs is a little bit of impetus to help happy customers to do something that most of them will be happy to do anyway.

3. **A referral capture process:** The manual process of collecting names over the counter, as in the dentist or optician example I mentioned earlier, is time-consuming and prone to error. I've heard some real horror stories of leads sitting in a box in the office and never being followed up. What you need is an automated way of making the offer to your existing clients, collecting the data and distributing the invitation to the lead.

The main task is to find a way of linking the prospect's information when it arrives with the person who recommended they get in touch. Ideas include things like affiliate links, unique offer codes, data capture widgets on websites, a list of names on a form or simply asking where they heard about you. The key is to collate the information automatically and have a process in place to manage the follow-up stages that come next.

When **Dropbox** launched in 2008, they offered customers additional storage if they referred their friends and business contacts. Within 12 months they had increased their users by 4000% by word of mouth alone, without a single penny being spent on other external advertising.

Their business model and referral schemes are incredibly simple. They give users 500mb of cloud storage space (a generous amount, but quickly consumed) for free. Users can upgrade to a paid account whenever they need to, but if they refer others, who start by creating a free account, they get a further 500mb for themselves. It is genius because all you are doing is giving your friend access to a valuable free account – there is absolutely no risk, and the important thing is that their service is brilliant.

On top of this, their sign-up process is painless and simple. You just enter your friend's email in a box, and it generates an email 'from you' inviting them to join - simple and completely transparent. With a couple more clicks, you could even send an email invite to multiple friends or every contact in your Gmail database. Dropbox even had the foresight to limit a referrer's free space to 16gb – they had to start making money at some point.

How to create a referral marketing campaign

Here is a practical bit for you. I'll describe it in steps 1-5, but it will be no surprise to you that I consider this to be a cycle too. So, when you have completed the five steps, you simply go back to the beginning and continue to tweak and develop the process.

Step 1: Set a SMART goal for your campaign (specific, measurable, achievable, realistic and timed). It should indicate the results you want from the actions that you take: in this case, that means how many referrals you need to gather. And the more specific your goal, the better your planning is likely to be. A typical goal might look something like this:

- **Specific:** I need to generate 100 new leads
- **Measurable:** the referrals will come through a specific link to identify them as unique from other leads
- **Achievable:** I have 500 existing clients, so 1 referral from 5 clients is a reasonable expectation
- **Realistic:** version one of this campaign worked last year, so this new, improved version should be a success
- **Timed:** the campaign will run for 4 weeks, and I expect to hit the target by then

Step 2: Choose the right incentive. You should know your customers very well, so work out what they might want or even go and ask them. The more desirable or valuable a reward is or is perceived to be, the more likely you are to inspire them to pass you referrals. If you are using a dual premium (where both the referrer and the person being referred is receiving a reward), make sure the person being referred will be compelled to act as well.

Step 3: Make it simple. The thing that kills most great offers is complexity. The system behind it may be complex and sophisticated, but the offer itself must be simple and transparent. And the action you want them to take has got to be the simplest thing of all. Your viewer needs to quickly understand the offer, what you need them to do and how to do it. Complexity is your enemy.

Step 4: Create and share your landing pages. Your landing pages do not need to be elaborate, but they must look professional, attractive and appear trustworthy. Pay attention to colours and content. Do not try and be too clever, make sure the offer is clearly articulated, and there are multiple opportunities to 'press here' and pass on the details of their referral. And make sure that your landing pages are sharable (as you never know when a referral might turn into a referrer).

Step 5: Promote your programme. You'd be surprised how many campaigns never get off the starting block. Their owners have put significant amounts of time, thought, and effort into putting them together, but are frightened to press 'go'. One thing is for sure: the 80% perfect campaign that gets sent out will always win more business than the 95% perfect one that doesn't. And 100% perfect simply does not exist – so stop trying to find it.

Here are some of the things you can do to promote your campaign:

- Send emails to your list of existing businesses
- Get affiliates and long-term customers to email to their lists
- Place banners adverts on your website home page
- Add calls-to-action in your blogs and social media posts
- Create social posts and run ads in as many places as you can
- Find influencers in relevant communities and persuade (incentivise) them to promote your programme

CHAPTER 16:

THE FINAL FRONTIER ATTRACTION

How the Star Trek principle can change the world

I'd like to think this is the first book in the entire history of literature to follow a chapter on generating referrals with one about space and interplanetary travel. As final frontiers and innovations go, I'm happy to claim that accolade from this publication – if nothing else. But this is not just a randomly generated insert or an afterthought. The opportunities that space represents are central to why I wrote this book. And my sincere hope is that this chapter (along with Chapter 18: 108 and counting) inspire you to reach a similarly 'live life to the full' conclusion.

The relevance to referrals is that everything anyone has ever achieved has been influenced by someone else. There really is 'nothing new under the sun', and each new advancement in thinking or technology grew out of some form of referral. One man observed another's skill; he adapted it and taught his daughter; she invented a process to simplify the skill, and her sister's friend knew a way to double the output.

People only want what other people have got

Before the invention of moving pictures, no one ever wanted to go to the movies on a Saturday night. Before December 1994, there was not a child alive who asked for a PlayStation for Christmas. And at least half the people reading this book will remember a time when we could survive for more than a few hours without looking at our smartphones. So, you can see that innovation and advancement, from the earliest civilisations (and before) through to today (and beyond), came about because of a type of referral. At the very least a passing on of the message. And just as in the sales circuit we've been studying and learning about in this book: referrals are an effective way to generate collaborations, improvements, growth, wealth and foundations.

And the beauty of this principle, using space as a metaphor, is that you can dream up ideas that don't exist and bring them into reality. There is no limit to space, and there is no limit to what you can imagine and pass on to others.

A great example of this is Star Trek, the most famous sci-fi series of all time. The brainchild of former US Air Force pilot Gene Roddenberry, Star Trek's first episode launched in September 1966, and it quite literally changed the world. It is quite conceivable; some would say a certainty, that at least some of the technology we see as commonplace today wouldn't exist if not for his vision.

From flip-top mobile phones to ship-wide wi-fi; and universal translators to holo-decks; some would say these were predictions of the future – I would argue they were influences. And you could go back through Roddenberry's life and see numerous clues to the things that inspired his imagination; from piloting Boeing B-17 Flying Fortresses in WW2, to writing scripts for another 1960s series, The Lieutenant, where he met a certain Leonard Nimoy. Everything that happens tomorrow will be inspired by (and referred to as) the things of today and yesterday.

So, innovation is a kind of recurring sales circuit. And if you can start to view your life similarly: not as a journey, but as a circle of ongoing adjustments and improvements to increase the efficiency and value of the outcomes – surely you must be on to a good thing.

The world today and space tomorrow

I'm writing this book during the most significant world-changing event to occur since the second world war: The global Covid-19 pandemic that began to affect everyone's lives during the first half of 2020. (I didn't really want to mention the Coronavirus – but it is important for the context of the next part of the chapter.)

(Caveat: the next three paragraphs are written reservedly and conjecturally – at a point in time.) The major news channels in all major countries during the early and middle months of 2020 were focused almost entirely on internal news. International events were still covered (we do live in the internet age after all) and overseas video conferencing calls increased by the thousands. But, the majority of features were the problems at home. In fact, I found myself wondering from time to time what 'headline news' wasn't getting a single mention during those times.

Likewise, the governments of those same major nations seem to have been looking inwards. A famously toxic topic that had all-but consumed the corridors of power in the UK for several years suddenly seemed reduced to an undertone. The effect of the pandemic (and as I write this, I do not know how that particular story will end) has been to cause a rapidly globalising world to consider the benefits of going insular. I actually believe history will show that this trend started sometime before Covid-19 appeared. The desire to become self-sufficient and less dependent on outside resource has been bubbling for a while. I do not want to get political, but as an observation, it seems the reluctance to invest in NATO, the EU and other international 'clubs' or organisations is evidence of an increasingly go-it-alone mentality. Certainly, past eras of huge national debt, economic frailty and survival instincts kicking in show that to be the pattern.

While the rapid expansion of communication technology has made our big, wide world smaller and more accessible, it seems that globalisation is slowing down. For the same reasons listed above, big and small businesses alike are adopting an inward gaze. Even global conglomerates are turning introspective and looking to sure up their own assets and supply lines, seeking self-sufficiency and independence (from relying on external supplies). And even if you are reading this chapter a year or five after I wrote it and thinking that is not how it happened – I hope you'll agree that the following comparison is still valid.

All is not lost. I am an optimist, and I can see hope in the skies.

The planet might be restricting its growth – but space is still out there, and big-dreaming entrepreneurs are looking up. Governments have long had a presence and passing interest in the Space Race: but it is the wealth and vision of private enterprise that is accelerating the pace. Companies like Virgin Galactic, SpaceX, Blue Origin, Orion Span and Boeing are leading the way, and history seems to be repeating itself once more.

In the last great age of exploration, when countries and continents like America and Australia were discovered and colonised, it was independent industrialists who made it work. Taxes didn't build the New World and fund the Industrial Revolution – private enterprise did. Now, I am not condoning some of the horrible side effects and corrupt practices that were associated with those endeavours; and I hope that sort of evil is never seen upon the earth again. But the facts record that much of the world's wealth was born out of those pioneering feats. Great advances came out of the hardships too: technological innovations, the arts, industry, philosophy, architecture, culture and any great discoveries in nature.

New nations were born, and in a matter of a few hundred years, they sat among the richest on earth.

There are riches in the heavens

Who makes the most money from a gold rush? Think about it for a moment. Equally, I could ask who benefits the most from the national lottery each week. That's right, the winner – the one who strikes gold or whose numbers come up. But they are the exception to the rule – they are the headline, not the true story. Thousands of people are employed across the country by the organisations that run various lotteries and similar games of chance. Unlike the 'single' winner, their families are guaranteed an income. Similarly, the people who manufacture shovels, wheelbarrows, pans and pickaxes were the real winners when the gold-hungry hopefuls ran to the hills.

Everyone knows that Neil Armstrong was the first man on the moon, Buzz Aldrin was second and the other chap stayed on the spaceship. But in the same way that most forget the name of the third astronaut (Michael Collins) they tend to overlook the industry, innovation, investment and involvement of so many other people. It would be easy to call it a pointless and expensive publicity stunt, one-upmanship over the Russians or a waste of time. But the reality is that it created jobs, accelerated computerisation, increased our knowledge of the natural world and set the foundation for our modern world.

Without the competition induced by the Space Race of the 1960s, we may never have had the internet, GPS, iPads or electric cars. True, our passage towards global warming might be a little slower, but we would also be far more ignorant of its approach and less able to do something about it. My point is that you do not have to be an astronaut to benefit from the exploration of space. The world's potential is brighter if we look to the stars.

I will come back to this in more detail in Chapter 18 (where I explain why I will live to be 108 years old), but for now, let me leave you with this thought.

When the first human colonies are established on the Moon and Mars, who is going to provide the infrastructure? Yes, there will be a few people who live and work there in the early years – and the tourist industry will enjoy the boost. But what about all the practical things to be supplied by earthbound 'ordinary' people? Who is going to sort out the food supplies, manufacture clothing, manage real estate sales, legislate health and safety, set up supply chains, design living spaces, invent space-styled toiletries, manufacture new materials and build the cot for the first off-world baby ever born?

I believe we will need all of the above in my lifetime. And even if I miss out on some of it – I know for a fact that the second half of my life will be more expansive and altogether more adventurous for imagining the part I can play.

The potential of space takes you outside your normal frame of reference. By default, it forces you to think bigger and to see fewer restrictions. And if you get into the habit of thinking bigger about space – you will think bigger about everything else.

CHAPTER 17:

REPEAT PURCHASING

Build an 'existing customers only' community

We have arrived at number nine in our circuit of ten pitstops. And by all reasonable measures, you would expect that to mean we are getting near the end. But, of course, that is not the case with this circuit. As with each of the stops we've visited on the way here, this could just as easily be the beginning point. In fact, this stop is very much a start.

If I did not actually say it, then I certainly implied in chapter fifteen, that referrals are the easiest way to generate new business. Well, I apologise because I may have misled you. The easiest way to get new business is to get your existing customers to buy again or purchase new stuff. Why? Because they are already a customer and should already trust you and love you.

The end is only the beginning

I cannot think of too many business models where there is no upsell, cross-sell or repeat business opportunity. A few spring to mind where there may be an extended buying cycle (kitchens, cars and weddings) but even in those markets, there are complementary opportunities to be explored. Someone might only refurb their kitchen every ten years, but they could need a bedroom or box room in between. Getting a new car might only happen every three years, but at least it's predictable, and most households have at least two cars these days. And weddings should be once in a lifetime, but the reality is that they are not 50% of the time. And every couple has anniversaries, other celebrations and the patter of tiny feet come along at some point too. (There are, of course, friends and family to consider here also, but we covered that potential in the referrals chapter.)

In the majority of sectors, however, the need is regular and repeatable, and as long as it gets managed well is really easy to maintain. Let's take coaching or training, for example. Although we tend to joke about the spike in gym membership subscriptions every January and how they are transformed into a pointless direct debit by Easter, the truth is that most get cancelled. And even among serious fitness enthusiasts, personal trainers are astutely aware that their services are cyclical. Likewise, business coaches, life coaches; and other professions where the product is some sort of tutoring or support; tend to be a pay-as-you-go or limited time contract.

But the point is that the businesses providing these services are aware that is the case. They might not like it when a customer says, I'm going to take a break, and it may come as a surprise, but it shouldn't be. It is simply the nature of that type of business. But it doesn't mean that conversation has to be the end of the relationship.

The hard work to make the selling easy

Companies work hard to make sales. If selling were really easy, everyone would be running a successful business and retiring early to pursue their life's ambitions. Well, as I've established earlier in the book – selling is easy – if you are prepared to put in the hard work to make it so. But, if you have put in the hard work to find a customer and persuade that customer to part with their hard earned cash – surely you should make every effort to ensure your efforts are maximised, and the value for money exchange lasts as long as possible. And, if you know the cycle is going to happen; you can avoid the disappointment by being prepared.

Surprise, surprise: the answer is having a system. So, let's look at the personal trainer scenario again. A gym member, paying their general £19.99 per month decides to take on a personal trainer to help reach their goals quicker and more effectively. The trainer, knowing from years of experience that they can get visible results in three months, sets up the agreement. After three months, most trainers simply say, "goodbye – you know where I am if you need me". Some customers might say, "I loved that – please can I carry on" but most will wander off and put on weight or go somewhere else. What a missed opportunity!

If you know the usual behaviour of your customers (and you are expert at what you do so you should be able to get a good handle on the numbers), you can plan a strategy around keeping them interested. For example, our personal trainer could, at the point where their customer announces the inevitable rest period, ask if they would like to be sent a free weekly motivation programme by email. The first one of these might be a review of the progress they made during their training and then a series of pre-written and targeted messages designed to help them maintain focus. After a while (again, experience will dictate exactly when) an attractive offer could land in the customer's inbox with a reminder of the results of the previous programme.

If this sounds complicated, I promise you it isn't. Automating sequences is always far easier than it sounds, and the great thing is that you only have to do the work once – then the process simply pays you over and over again.

Turning £50 into £500 and £100 into £10,000

Let's imagine a couple spend £50 at a restaurant. It is local and convenient, but it is their first ever visit. They enjoy the food and the service and get up to leave thinking that they might visit again one day. But there are, of course, many other places looking for their business, so 'might' is hardly a reliable number. That scenario happens every Thursday, Friday and Saturday night in every town throughout the land. In some restaurants, however, there is a process in place to capture at least one of the couple's email address (and their permission to use it). It may be that they had to book online, filled in a 'how did we do' slip or the waiter simply asked if they could send them vouchers for the next time they visit. After receiving information about the restaurant's latest offer to enjoy a free bottle of wine when they come back within a month, the couple are treated to extra special care the next time. They are then happy to share information like their birth dates, and they start to feel at home. You can imagine what the savvy restaurant marketing team do a month before each birthday can't you? And when a 30th, 40th or similar anniversary comes along the offer will be even better. All the restaurant needs to do is set up a process and a system to make sure that each step happens.

If you think back to chapter fourteen (How I built EXELA: one small step and one reliable system at a time) and my own journey – systemising the repeat purchasing aspect is the absolute foundation of everything I do. It has allowed me the freedom to add multiple layers of income and opportunity within my business, released me from the day-to-day confines of doing the work, given me space to perfect other systems that run the business and means I can dream up exciting new projects to pursue.

If you think carefully about this, you will see that in your business there is an opportunity to turn a one-off new sale into a lifetime of repeat business. Then, instead of working incredibly hard, investing time and money to find leads, and giving it everything you've got to convert a £30 advert into a £100 sale, you can create a self-sustaining and automatically growing business. Your one-off sale of £100 could easily become a monthly contract, and that relationship could last ten years or more. All it takes is 10% more effort on top of the other nine steps in the sales circuit.

Let me give you one more example before finishing this chapter on explaining how easy it is to automate.

Supermarkets aren't silly

Why do you think we all have store cards in our possession? It is not because the stores want to give away even more of the extremely tight margins their mega empires are built upon. It is because to run a retail store in a highly competitive marketplace, you have no choice but to sell a lot of high volume, low margin, even loss leader items.

So, the supermarkets have developed highly sophisticated systems that automatically capture, measure, segment and manipulate the communications and offers that arrive at your door. It quite literally is the case that the system knows if you have stopped ordering something and it assumes you are going somewhere else to buy it. Likewise, if you start ordering a particular item, it will calculate that you might also need one of a range of complementary products that other shoppers often buy together. And it even has a database of the longer life products that people like to buy in bulk to save a few pennies. Consequently, the selection of offers you receive genuinely is totally bespoke to you – it is not just your name on the letter that is personalised.

Imagine the millions of customers that walk through those stores doors each week. Now think of the thousands of product lines that they stock so that they can fulfil the demand. Sounds complicated, doesn't it?

Well, here is the thing. It really is not that hard to do. And once the system has been set up, and all the rules and successive actions programmed in, it will look after everyone automatically and seamlessly. In a system of that complexity and detail, there will be people checking, measuring and tweaking the data daily: but in general terms, it works on its own. And that effort alone is why these national chains are able to maintain their position in the price, service and branding battles of modern retail.

Complexity is easy

The bottom line is that if you don't love your customers automatically (by that I mean through a process-driven system), someone else will. Most small businesses do not need a system anywhere near as involved as the ones supermarkets have to maintain. But if you have any number of clients and you want to maximise the longevity of those relationships you have to have a process. It doesn't even have to be automated: but it does need to have steps to follow and actions to follow, determined by the responses and buying habits of your customers.

When you think of the alternative – a hard-won customer choosing a competitor next time – then the effort of creating a repeat customer process suddenly looks like a necessity. Complexity is easy when the health of your business depends on it.

CHAPTER 18:

108 AND COUNTING

What you do today creates a better tomorrow

I didn't really have a mid-life crisis; I think I was always too busily focused on the next thing that I had to do in my well-planned path ahead. But I did have a defining moment on my 54th birthday. I don't mean to exaggerate or glorify the experience; it really was little more than a 'moment' in time when I decided I was halfway there. I suppose it was the first time I had stopped to think about the path for a while, and it just happened to be that day.

So, I decided that I was halfway through my life, and that meant that I would live to be 108. Let me explain a little more about that ambition and why it is so relevant to having a plan or circuit to follow for your life.

The average life expectancy for someone living in the UK in 1960 was 71: by 1980 it was 74. It rose to 78 in 2000 and today is around 81 years old. If the average life expectancy increases by 3-4 years every 20 years, that takes you to the lower 90s by the time I reach 108. But when you factor in that 'average' accounts for everyone who dies younger than that number (including the tragically young), the extraordinary recent advancements in medical technology, and the fact that I have already reached more than halfway in good health – I think my estimation is totally reasonable.

But whether you buy into my calculation and intuition or not – please don't miss my point. I have created a plan that I am going to follow for the rest of my life – and you can/should do the same.

Quarter three and counting

This is where I get quite excited by the prospect of planning my long and opportunity-filled life ahead. Even as I have been writing this book and thinking about the life-circuit that brought me to this point, it occurred to me that life can be broken up into four segments for most people.

1. **Finding my feet:** The first quarter of my life I was trying to work it all out and discover the best fit for my skills, interests, and ambitions. I studied, travelled, and tried out various jobs; I gathered a bunch of skills and experiences, and finally settled into family life and a career (of sorts).

   You could think of that stage of life like gathering leads, getting a quote and making an offer.

2. **Building on the foundation:** The next quarter I spent starting a family, honing my business craft,

learning the life/work balance equation, setting down roots, building stability and income, and becoming a version of me I was satisfied with.

That stage could be described as mastering the sales process and generating more leads or maximising my opportunities.

3. **Branching out once more:** Perhaps I am fortunate to have built a business that generates enough income, with or without me, to fund an adventure. At the risk of patting myself on the back, however; I believe that 95% of the people fortunate enough to be born in this country could do the same. If you are a 'quarter one' person reading this book, I hope you can see that. If you are in 'quarter two', I hope you are doing the same. And if you are in 'quarter three', I want to inspire you to embrace it. If you are in 'quarter four' good on you – I'd love to know how you are doing.

With what I have learned, the things I have done and a solid foundation beneath me, I have big plans for this quarter. I am going to approach opportunities like a galactic traveller. My approach will be that there is no box, no limit and no stone unturned in making the most of every minute of every day before me. I am halfway through, but that is still a lot of time in which to achieve, experience and explore.

The stage I am currently venturing into is like long term nurture and client onboarding; it is about reviewing and passing on what I know.

4. **Reaping the reward:** What a thrill to think of what might be possible by the time I reach the final quarter. I don't know what to expect, but my imagination has already been there and, while I am in no rush to leave my current stage on the life-circuit, I will embrace it when it comes.

The last stage has a feeling of referrals and repeat purchase about it. By then, my family will include grand-children, great-grand-children and lots of love. I intend to pass on the value that I have acquired and help guide them on well-planned circuits of their own. I might even write a few more memoirs.

Recalibrate and go for it

There will be people reading this book who take a cynical view of this chapter – I hope that is not you. Others will feel inspired by it, some might garner a little regret. Whatever you are feeling, please do this, right now. Go and recalibrate.

All measurement instruments need to be recalibrated every now and then. Thermometers, speedometers, scales, hydrometers, seismometers, clocks, and life plans all need checking to see if they still measure up to the standard. So, take some time out, perhaps even put this book down for a while and grab a notebook (I won't be offended); and decide where you are in your lifecycle. Whatever the time, there is a high proportion chance that you have a lot of time left. Decide how much time you have left to play with – and plan to make it count.

Perhaps a sports analogy might help. In my case, on my 54th birthday, I went into the dressing room for a half-time team talk. I looked at my first-half performance and saw that I was 3-1 up. That meant I could play with a little more swagger in the second half. Allow myself a little more freedom, let my creative side flourish and look to finish strongly. Of course, I had to keep an eye on the defence and sure up my backline, as even the strongest teams can get caught on the break. But my intention is to push forward and increase my margin of victory.

You might look at your halftime score and feel it is all even with all to play for, or maybe you find yourself a goal down at the break. But here is the rub! You only get one chance at this. There is still a whole second half to play. What have you got to lose? Imagine the heroic headline as your comeback gets going. And if you are still playing in your first half, my advice is to push hard and make sure you go in strong to give yourself the best shot at a cup-winning final whistle.

So, go back and work out how you got to this point, what you can afford to do next, the things that you would like to do in the future, how you might be able to make that possible and who you are going to bring on the journey with you. Do not waste today or any of the day you have left. Treat it like a space quest. Dream big, plan smart and take small steps towards that plan today.

CHAPTER 19:

BUILD A LEAD BANK

Back to the top

10

Build a Lead Bank

In one sense, we have arrived at the end of the sales circuit: number ten of ten steps is building a lead bank. But, as I have alluded to previously, there really isn't an end, or a beginning; as all the steps form part of a perpetual journey. In fact, if you were paying attention as I described the four stages of my lifecycle in the last chapter, you may have noticed that I included 'gathering' leads at the beginning of my description of stage one.

I suggested that nothing starts until you get that first click. But in reality, you need leads in order to persuade someone to click. And often that means someone will have had to refer your services after enjoying a great experience themselves. But that could only have happened as a result of you making them feel welcome as a customer, nurturing the relationship of making them a sales offer. The truth is that the sales cycle could start anywhere, and its success depends on you keeping the various processes turning and feeding each other.

The real magic, however, starts at this point. Once the machine is ticking over and producing positive, profitable and rewarding results for your business, you can set about fine-tuning and amplifying. We have addressed the concept of fine-tuning several times through the various stages, and I'll touch on that again shortly, but what I really want to focus in this chapter is filling the bucket.

Turning on the tap

In chapter five, I spoke about keeping an eye on leaks and regularly checking to make sure the system is capturing and actioning data in the correct way. As long as there is a routine in place to do this, your job at this stage is simply to keep increasing the number of leads. Think about it: if you had built a machine that (legally) pumped out twenty-pound notes each time you put a five-pound note in the slot, what would you be doing all day? I hope that by now, your answer isn't simply to find as many five-pound notes as you can and feed the machine. My approach would be to hire someone to borrow five-pound notes on the promise of paying the lender six pounds in return and then pay the collector £2 per collection. I would then pay someone else £1 per shot to fill the machine and a third employee the same to collect the twenties and deliver them to my 'next project' account.

Once you have your fully automated, remotely managed sales circuit up and running, you simply need to find a way to fill it with as many leads as possible.

One thing to watch here is capacity. Leaks and other problems occur in a sales circuit for several reasons. Sometimes it is just a case of software glitches, gremlins, other unidentifiable causes, or human error – which is why you need to check and test it on a regular basis. Other times, it is because a particular thing has changed. Maybe your marketing is no longer effective, or the need in the market has shifted. There are so many outside influences that will stop a previously smooth running and efficient system from delivering.

But as a business looks to grow, the biggest thing to watch is overloading its capacity to deliver. It is possible for a business to 'grow broke' if you have not paid enough attention to managing the cashflow. Or, perhaps the extra demand is slowing down delivery and service quality to such an extent that customers are being let down or neglected. Remember, any system is only as strong as its weakest link – and you need to be aware of all the opportunities for things to go wrong before you start to scale.

A simple checklist is usually enough to manage the consistency and robustness of your sales circuit – but it must be used regularly. When it comes to the marketing, sales and attracting leads elements a good strategy to employ is split testing or AB testing.

Split testing

This is the concept of trying different marketing approaches on the same body of leads to see which is more effective in converting sales. Let's assume you have a database of 1000 potential leads and you have created a brand-new piece of marketing to send them. The marketing department is typically excited and believes that their work is brilliant and inspired. But, of course they love it – they created it. What they think is irrelevant, however. Only the lead base can tell you for sure if what they have put together will work.

So, you have two choices. You either send out the 5000 letters and hope that the work is as compelling and perfectly aimed as your (slightly more nervous at the prospect of the approaching send button) marketing team claim it to be. Or you can test it first. The way you do this is select two groups of 50 leads and call them Set A, and Set B. Then ask the marketing team to go and make a few amendments to the marketing piece, or maybe even produce a second idea altogether. With the two test cases in hand, you send out one version to Segment A and the other version to Segment B – each group with a different 'claim' code so that you can measure the results as they come.

Then you simply pick the piece that performs better and use that version. If you want to further maximise the impact of the activity, you could even try another test on two new sets of 50 leads by creating tweaked versions of the winning campaign. There is an argument for continuing to test and measure, but you risk falling into the trap of never sending anything until it reaches perfection. In the end 'good enough is good enough'.

Amplification and automation

Here are a few tips on how to create a never-ending bank of leads to keep feeding into your smoothly running sales machine.

1. **Profiling:** I've mentioned avatars throughout the book and the concept of finding your ideal customer. When you start on your journey to identify the very best customers for your business and the ones who will benefit the most from what you do, it is largely guesswork. As you start to build a client base, it becomes clearer who is a good customer and who is (quite frankly) a bit of a burden. Eventually, you get to a point where the identification process becomes quite scientific, and it is more of a profiling exercise. You simply look at your top 20% of clients and amalgamate all their characteristics into one identity.

Then you address all your marketing to that identity (think of it as a company).

2. **Social content:** We live in an increasingly online, digital world where advertising, communication and feedback are highly social and shareable. The simple maths dictates that the more you put yourself out there, the more people (your ideal future customers) are going to be able to find you. The proviso here is, of course, that it has to be good quality and it has to be relevant to the people whose attention you are trying to reach. Everything that you put out there (blogs, videos, downloads, articles, how-to guides, and opinions) reflects your brand and your profile. It all needs to be strategically planned and congruent with a central message. As with the sales circuit itself, the central rule of content creation is quality first – volume second.

3. **Referrals and testimonials:** I have covered these topics in previous chapters, but it would be remiss not to mention them again here. The best source of pre-qualified, brand new leads comes from the people who already love what you do. Nothing could be stronger than that in terms of winning new business. In sales cycle terms, it is like going straight to 'GO' collecting £200 (or whatever the current Monopoly equivalent is) and starting the circuit again.

4. **Networking:** depending on what sort of business you are in, there are great opportunities to increase your lead base by getting out there and meeting people. In most towns and regions in the UK, there are strong business networking communities, and

it might be that one or another could work for you. From the more extensive national networks like the Federation of Small Businesses and various Chambers of Commerce, through to the local BNI, 4N and independent networking groups. These don't work for everyone, but I always suggest that business owners try – you never know until you have given things a go.

The big goal is to create a strategic and process-driven sales circuit that functions well, generates sales, is easily maintained and can be automated. Then you can step back and ask yourself the golden, entrepreneurial question: What shall I do next?

The answer to that question is a personal one and depends on where you are in your lifecycle and where you want to go with your life. For me, business is great, and I love what I do. It has always been a passion in my life. But I also recognise, particularly as I recalibrated upon entering my third quarter, that it is a means to an end and there is much more out there to discover and enjoy.

What do you want to do next?

CHAPTER 20:

RINSE AND REPEAT

Shampoo, space and other stories...

In this chapter, I want to share a few stories of systems that work well in the world of business, sports, and nature. The first is the apocryphal tale of the US marketing Ad-Man who doubled his company's sales in just three words.

The ultimate repeat purchase story

The story goes that a shampoo company in the 1950s was struggling to maintain sales and looked like it wouldn't last another six months. It was in the days where people washed their hair 2-3 times per week, rather than every day as is the modern trend, and the preference was for products that held the hair in place. The Managing Director was out of ideas after yet another store had cancelled one of their regular orders. That weekend an old school friend came round for dinner and was talking about the success of his firm's latest advertising success. In a desperate last throw of the dice, the shampoo boss asked if he would come up with few ideas to try and save his business.

Two days later, his friend came back, clutching a tiny piece of paper and holding back an enormous smile. "I think you might like this" he said. The piece of paper revealed just three words: rinse and repeat. The Managing Director looked at it for a long five minutes, first trying to work out what it meant and then imagining the possibilities.

And that, according to legend, is why you washed your hair twice this morning and how a hair products company doubled its sales overnight.

The death-defying sales circuit

Regardless of your interest in football or the colours of the team you follow, few would disagree with the phenomenal achievements built by Sir Alex Ferguson at Manchester United. His success is impressive indeed, but only made possible, if truth be told, by the legacy laid down by another Scottish Knight of the Realm a few decades earlier.

After a successful career playing for both Manchester City and Liverpool, Alexander Matthew Busby became the manager of Manchester United in 1945. It was just after the second world war and, while it was a professional sport in every sense of the word, it inhabited a very different commercial environment to the one we recognise today.

But, from day one Busby, fresh out of the army, started to apply process, system and ambition to everything the club did. In 1948 the club had won the FA Cup (its first trophy in 37 years) and established itself as a top-three side in the league before winning the title in 1952.

And here is what he did. He created a system of deliberate, professional training standards; introduced a strategy of established players alongside youngsters (often just 16 or 17 having been scouted from school) and framed the whole regime with discipline. He even insisted on being allowed the final say on any players the team signed: an unprecedented situation in those days when the board made all financial decisions. To top it all, he sold his plan to the owners of the club and secured himself a unique five-year contract that would allow him to complete the first revolution of his success cycle.

The infamous and tragic Munich air crash of February 1958 that killed eight first-team players and ended the playing careers of two more would have destroyed any ordinary football club. Devastated and barely escaping with his own life, however, Busby chose to honour those who lost their lives by carrying on. And such was the strength of the system that he had built; he was able to do so. Even with those catastrophic physical and emotional barriers to overcome, Manchester United won the FA Cup again in 1963, football league title in 1965 and 1967, before going on to become the first English club to lift the European Cup in 1968.

The perpetual contribution of the butterfly

If you were going to look for an example of growth through a life cycle, the butterfly is an obvious place to start. But the predictability of the metaphor does not take away the lessons that can be observed in terms of the sales cycle. You see, setting up an automated circuit to build your business is all about taking a lead from one stage to another and benefiting from its changes in size shape and value. And, just like the butterfly, the end result should always be the start of a new cycle.

Let's look at the four stages of a butterfly life cycle in detail:

1. **Eggs:** The adult butterfly usually lays its eggs on the leaves of plants. This creates good environmental conditions and helps maintain the right levels of heat, light, moisture and protection from the elements. It also gives the defenceless unborns half a chance of avoiding the attention of predators. Like the leads that you are gathering for your sales circuit, there is little more you can do in the early stages than to let them know there is an environment available that might be of future value to them. Every customer you now have and each one you are yet to win started off as an unhatched lead that needed feeding and nurturing.

2. **Caterpillars:** In many ways, it is still a mystery to science that such a thing as metamorphosis occurs. Rather than becoming a baby version of its parent,

like 99% of nature, the butterfly starts its active life as something else altogether. And, if you consider the stages of the sales circuit that we have discussed in this book, you'll see there are rarely any shortcuts in the process. A lead becomes a conversation before they turn into a customer – and those are two very different things. Depending on the species of butterfly, their caterpillar can live anywhere from a few weeks to several years – and all they do in that time is eat.

Likewise, there are various stages described in the sales circuit where all you are doing is feeding your leads with information that will build them into a customer. In fact, the adult butterfly will choose the leaf to lay its eggs on specifically because it is one that is good to eat. Targeted marketing works in every area of life.

3. **Chrysalis:** The life expectancy of a caterpillar is not actually all that favourable. Only a small percentage of them actually make it to the pupal stage. And that is exactly why client onboarding and nurturing is so critically important. Every market sector is different: but for most that will employ a fully automated sales to conversion system, it is because large numbers are needed to win a result. For example, if you need to win 10 new deals a month and your conversion rate is 2%, you need to generate 500 leads. That is a lot of new contacts to make and a huge effort – so you should treat everyone who says 'yes' as an incredibly valuable new 'life'.

The transformation that takes place in a chrysalis is both beautiful and mind blowing. I suppose my analogy seems small and insignificant by comparison, but I have built a fantastic life and future opportunity for myself and my family by embracing the sales circuit. And you can too.

4. **Butterflies:** The thing about butterflies is that they attract attention. And, while they are beautiful to look at, this attention has a highly practical function. Like the proactive sharing of referrals and testimonials in the sales circuit described in this book, the purpose of a butterfly's colourful wings is to ensure that its story doesn't stop there. The lifecycle of a butterfly depends on more eggs being generated and others having the same opportunities that it had.

In your business, the single best way to build a successful business is to view each converted sale as an opportunity to nurture a testimonial.

CHAPTER 21:

WHAT ABOUT YOU?

After all – that is why you are reading this book!

So, as we come to the close of this book, I want to throw a question across to you. What are you going to do about it? I am not Bill Gates, Alan Sugar or Richard Branson, any more than I am Lionel Messi, Lewis Hamilton or Anthony Joshua. My wealth, influence and success pale into insignificance compared to people like that. But, maybe that is why you should pay a little more attention to the story in these pages. I'm not suggesting that what the 1% of the 1% have achieved is unachievable for ordinary people: rather that you can aim for the stars and enjoy the moon.

In this book, I have shared elements of my personal story, alongside other metaphors and ideas that highlight the way that life works in cycles. I hope I have also blended those stories with enough practical information and education to help you start building your sales circuit. My intention was never to write a textbook or a 'how to' manual (my courses and online training products do that), but to inspire you to achieve business success on purpose and with a bigger goal. In these pages, we have travelled back in time, across continents, into corporate and entrepreneurial life, through sports stories, to the stars and safely back to earth. And it has ended up with you.

My team and the training courses I have created can teach you more about setting up, scheduling and fine-tuning automated sales circuits on systems such as Keap and Infusionsoft. But I cannot make you do anything if you don't muster up the drive to act. I genuinely believe that anyone reading this book has the opportunity to sales circuit themselves to their version of space travel.

What if?

The beauty of thinking about space is that it forces you to let go of boundaries and the things that you know. It forces you to think 'what if' and to imagine 'what might be'.

Did you know that the first electric cars were being built 200 years ago? People like Hungarian inventor, Ányos Jedlik, who built a small electric vehicle in 1828 and Scottish engineer, Robert Anderson, who developed a more advanced model in 1932. From the 1870s to the early 1900s, the idea became quite popular; but eventually, the range, reliability and cost-effectiveness of the combustion engine put the industry asleep for a while. But what if the idea had persisted? Would the planet be better off now?

If you look back through political, commercial, cultural and every personal history, you could ask 'what if' a billion times and come up with millions of alternative outcomes. The practice is probably pointless because you cannot change the past. What if Blockbuster had bought Netflix when it had the opportunity in the year 2000? How did twelve publishers come to reject the first Harry Potter script? How big would Kodak be now if they had launched the first digital camera, invented by one of their own engineers in 1975? And what if Winston Churchill had died of pneumonia, aged 11, as was so very nearly the case?

I get that some people reading this book will have grown up with very little and others perhaps surrounded by a few more trappings of their parents' wealth. But I am also confident of the fact that most readers will have been born in the Western world and, whether they fully appreciate it or not, are fortunate enough to be surrounded by opportunity. For example, 99% of the people born in the UK have access to basic education and a roof over their head. My point is that whatever your circumstances today, the things that have happened to you in the past, or the cares and concerns that may face you tomorrow; you can ask 'what if' today.

What if you choose to recognise that time is in limited supply but that you still have a lot left to utilise. What if your assessment that you are 2-1 down at half time inspires a memorable comeback that will inspire a generation? What if you decide to stop looking at the dust, wondering what life has to offer you, and choose to reach for the stars and see what is out there?

I'm not suggesting that any of the above is easy or that you can miraculously conjure an overnight success out of thin air. In fact, I am advocating exactly the opposite.

I'm challenging you to put in the hard work that it takes to make the selling easy. If you decide to start creating a process-driven, strategically designed sales system for your business today, you might find that you can retire in five years and start pursuing your dreams. You might be able to do that - if that is what you want. The one thing that I know for sure is that if you decide not to change anything or make anything better, the days will keep on ticking by and eventually run out just the same.

Back to the sales circuit:

To finish this book, I want to summarise the ten steps of the sales circuit and the main practical takeaways for each one.

1. **Get a quote:** Every lead that arrives on your website is there because they want something. Remember that fact and respond to it. Give them an action they can follow. Offer them a button to click and create an opportunity to move them to the next stage of the process.

   "Visitors want something (price, information, guidance, news, comparison). So, respond to what they want"

2. **Make an offer:** This is the interface between marketing and sales (or passive and proactive selling). And while it sits at number two in the circuit and is in the middle of the sales pipeline it is perhaps the most important switch in the circuit. The offer is the

gatekeeper to making money and separates the leads that will convert from the ones that are simply leads.

If you do not make an offer to your leads, they will never know how to take the next step in the circuit that you have designed for them. Your business will need a series of offers to attract various types and mindsets of lead. They could include the following:

- Let's have a chat: an offer does not need to cost money, it could be as simple as booking a call so that you can work out what the lead wants (and in listening to them you are building their trust)

- Telephone consultation: the next step up from an informal chat on the phone is a consultation with an agenda to fix or consult on a specific topic. They can choose, or you can dictate what is covered in these consultations

- Meeting: similar to the formal consultation, a face-to-face or online meeting would be another way to address specific issues a lead might have and share some of your wisdom or insight

- Product demo: if you are selling software you could demo the product online, or a product could be shown in person – potential customers love to get their hands on a product and try-before-they-buy

- Webinar: increasingly popular, webinars are a great way to gather a crowd of hungry leads in one place, create an idea of mass demand and share your expertise with an audience

- Seminar: similar to webinars, these are an excellent way of building credibility in the space where you work and showing your leads that working with you (buying your products) is a great idea

- Tripwire purchase: most people would easily part with £9.99 to get a small trial product, try something out or purchase a how-to guide from an industry expert – these tripwire purchases serve to fit two purposes: capturing details and proving that a lead is prepared to pay you for something

- Full purchase: in some industries and sectors, the nature of the product means that a full purchase is a natural progression from entering the lead pool – if that is the case, you still need be proactive and ask them to buy

3. **Sales process:** If the offer stage is 'the gatekeeper' to making money, the bottom half of the sales pipeline is where the transaction takes place. From here, it is all about conversion and ensuring that as many offers as possible come back with a result (preferable a sale). Unless there is a result here (and one that you can consistently tweak and improve), the whole circuit is a complete waste of time and effort.

Here is a summary again of the four-stage sales process:

Stage one: Qualification: deciding which leads are the right ones and are worth pursuing

Stage two: Discovery: opening up the sales conversation; fact-finding, answering questions and further qualification

Stage three: Bidding: proposing details of the solution (how and what it is) and pitching the cost to the customer

Stage four: Closing: closing the deal, negotiating the terms and agreeing on the scope of the work

4. **Lead generation:** for most people, the sales journey stops at stage three, with the money in the bank. But the sales circuit is all about creating a lifetime (or for as long as you want the process to run) of recurring and self-generating leads and customers. The more you perfect the circuit and the more leads you feed into it, the smoother and more efficiently it will continually and perpetually run.

Leads are generated by adhering to the basic rules of marketing:

- Identify your target market – who they are and how to contact them
- Craft a message that is addressed to them personally

- Decide the best media (often multiple places at once) to amplify your message

Remember, that to capture leads effectively, you need bait and a net. We refer to these functions as lead magnets (reports, checklists, eBooks and samples), and lead capture mechanisms (landing pages, emails and forms).

5. **Long term nurture:** your lead bank now contains a long list of names, at varying positions within the sales circuit. Your lead bank is actually your entire list – customers, leads and lapsed customers alike. Of course, you must learn to segment your list and communicate with them according to your relationship, but the key is to keep the communication alive and well.

In the very basic terms, your job is to tell them things that are interesting and useful. Each market sector is as different and varied as each customer on your list, but that is why you must travel the circuit diligently. The more circuits you complete, the more you learn to understand what they want to know.

The ultimate objective is to introduce yourself to the strangers on your list, turn those you've met into friends, and invite your friends to become raving fans. This is a nurture stage – not a sales stage – and that means you are simply sharing value. Some of the best nurture tools include:

- Articles
- Blog posts

- Videos
- Tutorials
- How-to guides
- Quizzes and questionnaires
- Calculators
- Resources
- Courses

6. **Client Onboarding:** the key to stopping a first-time sale from becoming a one-time sale is client onboarding. If you promise every new customer a level eight service, knowing that your standard is a ten, you will always delight them. If you show them that you value their order and appreciate their loyalty, even before they have given it, you will have a good chance of retaining it.

Making it easy to buy the first time will encourage a repeat purchase. Creating an outstanding first use experience, with support, instruction, additional services, and a full guarantee will ensure that if anything does go wrong, they will continue to love you. And if you keep a relationship that started with an outstanding first impression going at the same standard, you are well on your way to winning a friend and a fan.

Doing business well is not hard – it just takes attention and a little more effort than most people give.

7. **Reviews & Testimonials:** in a perfect world, every satisfied customer should go and tell three more people like themselves that you are the best in the world. But in the real world that does not happen.

Some happy customers will enthusiastically recommend you whenever they have the chance. Almost every other happy customer you have will be equally happy to recommend you (that fact is fundamental to remember), but they will need a little encouragement to do it.

Whether it is a simple link and a request for the testimonial, or an incentivised campaign, you must make the effort to make these happen.

8. **Referrals:** Just like reviews and testimonials, referrals will not happen on their own, so you need to set up an effective process to generate this action. Why spend the majority of your marketing budget on campaigns to identify, find, warm up and then convert new leads into sales but neglect the easy option? It makes no sense.

A good referral system takes all of the hard work and expense out of generating new leads (many of which are likely to be the best quality leads you could ever have). Again, like the review and testimonial gathering exercise – an incentivised campaign with your happy customers is a great way to reward their loyalty and to generate new leads.

9. **Repeat purchasing:** there is only one way to generate income for your business than through a qualified referral, and that is a repeat order. While so many big companies focus on 'new customers only' campaigns to attract new business, the smart ones look after their existing customers first. The logic here is not only defensive and hold on to what you

have got (although that is an incredibly smart and cost-efficient business strategy). It is equally about fulfilling an important stage in the sales cycle: namely, creating good customers who share the news.

Repeat purchasing clients are the best clients in the world. And the more of these that form the foundation of your business, the more likely that you can start looking to the stars and beyond for your next expansion, diversification or completely new project.

For most customers, a simple keep-in-touch campaign will keep your product and service top of mind and show them that you care. But do not limit this to emails. Test and measure, mix things up and send exciting and useful information through a variety of media. You could consider physical mail, making a telephone call, personalised videos, or vouchers.

10. **Build a lead bank:** once you have set up the sales cycle and put in place a process of continually testing, tweaking and improving, you are ready to fly. All you need to do is keep adding as many leads as your delivery system can handle and then grow.

This isn't just a case of amplification of your current marketing efforts. There are new markets and sectors to explore, alternative approaches to the same audience, trying other media to see if you have missed anyone out and ongoing improvement in your messages and value.

The important thing to remember as you go through each of these stages, from one to ten and back to one, is that the more you process and automate the smother and more effective it will be.

Then, and only then, will you be free to reach for the stars and dream.

P.S. Can I help you?

If you have enjoyed my story and learned anything from the insights and lessons I shared along the way, perhaps there might be a bit more I can help you with.

It will come as no surprise to you that I love technology. But you might be interested to know that it doesn't always take the highest spec, the fastest speed or a mountain of megabytes to grab my attention. I'm interested in finding technical solutions to simplify systems and maximise outcomes. And sometimes that means nothing more than the intelligent use of a clipboard and pen at an exhibition stand. That is far more effective than a dozen iPads, I promise you. Technology should make life simple.

Some of my favourite tricks, tips and tools

- As you will have read in the book, I have worked with a company called Keap for over 15 years. Their CRM (Customer Relationship Management) system and marketing automation tools are the best I have seen anywhere in the marketplace. They have two versions of the product: Keap aimed at 2-5 person businesses and Infusionsoft for larger organisations. In my opinion, you cannot do better to accelerate and automate your marketing than look at these solutions – and if you need any help, please get in touch with one of my team: https://exela.co.uk

- You can now expand Infusionsoft's email capability to include SMS and voice calls using an innovative extension called FYF (Fix Your Funnel). We find this supercharges reach and response rates by quite some margin.

- Another of my favourites is CustomerHub. If your offering includes any type of membership site or content sharing portal, this could be the perfect platform for you. It is a straightforward, hosted website giving you the capability to have members log-in and see personalised content. In my business, we use CustomerHub to help clients create paid courses and run virtual exhibitions.

- Zapier is like the magic wand of application technology. It is the cabling that connects applications together and means you no longer need to 'bend' applications to do jobs they were not designed to do. Instead, you can select the best tool for the job and let Zapier zap the data between applications. No manual handling or coding required – it is so simple.

And there's more...

These are just a handful of the dozens of tools we use and recommend for our customers each day. But a section like this often goes out of date quickly, especially when committed to print.

So, if you would like to keep up to date with my latest reviews and recommendation for Marketing Technology so you can maximise your automation and scale-up your results, visit: https://exela.co.uk

You will find a comprehensive list of tools on the resources menu, and if you need individual help, you can get in touch with one of my team. Just mention that my book sent you their way and they'll be delighted to help.

Happy automating
David

Lightning Source UK Ltd.
Milton Keynes UK
UKHW021632160920
370012UK00008B/205